BARRY
1935–1996
CRUMP

Dedication
to
Barry Crump

BARRY CRUMP
A TRIBUTE TO CRUMPY
1935–1996

Hodder Moa Beckett

NOTE FROM THE PUBLISHERS

Hodder Moa Beckett is proud to have this opportunity to pay tribute to Barry Crump. He was an extraordinary New Zealander who touched many lives, and entertained us for more than 30 years with his books. His contribution to our national iconography is immeasurable.

He was an enigma whose life has left more unanswered questions than explanations. This book is not intended as a definitive portrait of Crumpy, although it is a view of the private man behind the public facade. As his friends and family explain, Barry was a complex man who had countless adventures and moved in many social circles. Sometimes recollection of events is blurred, or contradictory. We have not attempted to reconcile varying accounts. One thing is certain, Barry was far from perfect, but to his close friends he was the best mate a person could wish for.

Barry enjoyed nothing more than a good yarn and he was consummate at the art of capturing an audience with stories and jokes. *Tribute to Crumpy* is a yarning session with people who knew Barry at different times in his life, and an opportunity for all of us to share a glimpse of a unique New Zealander.

EDITOR'S NOTE:

Wherever possible the spelling of names of people mentioned in this book has been checked for accuracy. The publishers apologise for any inaccuracies which may have inadvertently occurred.

Please note the spelling of Robin Lee Robinson's name as Robyn throughout the book. All contributors, and Barry himself, spelt her name this way. We have allowed it to stand to avoid confusion. As the letter on page 180 indicates, this has been a subject of discussion for some time. Sorry Robin!

ISBN 1-86958-584-4

© Hodder Moa Beckett Publishers Ltd
© Barry Crump – all extracts from books and writing as credited

Reprinted in limp edition 1997

First published in 1996 by Hodder Moa Beckett Publishers Limited
[a member of the Hodder Headline Group]
4 Whetu Place, Mairangi Bay, Auckland, New Zealand

Colour separation by Digital River
Printed by Bookbuilders, Hong Kong

All rights reserved. No part of this publication may be reproduced or transmitted in any form or by any means, electronic or mechanical, including photocopying, recording, or any information storage and retrieval system, without permission in writing from the publisher.

ACKNOWLEDGEMENTS

Hodder Moa Beckett would like to thank Maggie Crump for her support of this book, and her help and encouragement in compiling it. We are especially grateful for access to Crumpy's notebooks, address book and photograph collection. The colour photos featured throughout the book of landscapes, clouds, houses, letterboxes and farm scenes were all taken by Barry.

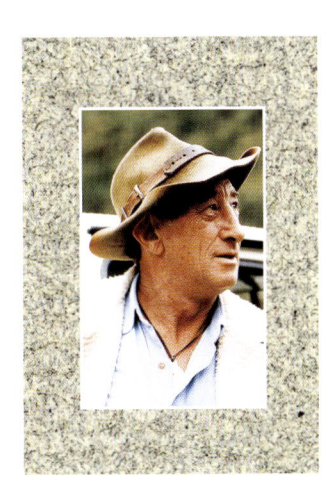

We appreciate the generosity of Barry Crump's friends and family who have shared their memories with us, and allowed us to reproduce their photographs. A special thank you to Alex King for the opportunity to print so many of Barry's letters to him.

Thanks to editorial consultant Kirsten Warner for interviewing many of the people featured in the book, and for capturing their voices.

CONTENTS

FOREWORD
BY
MAGGIE CRUMP
9

INTRODUCTION
BY
COLIN HOGG
13

CHAPTER 1
ONE OF US
30

BILL CRUMP*
COLIN CRUMP*

CHAPTER 2
A GOOD
KEEN MAN
46

SELWYN BUCKNELL*
JACK LASENBY*
KEVIN IRELAND
RAY RICHARDS

CHAPTER 3
A GOOD
KEEN GIRL
79

TINA LESTER*
MARTIN CRUMP*
ANDREW CAMPBELL
JEAN WATSON
JANET VANDA LYNDON
SIMONE RAINGER*
ROBIN LEE ROBINSON
MAGGIE CRUMP
JETHRO CRUMP
SIMON CRUMP
ANTON CRUMP
STEW NICHOLSON

CONTENTS

CHAPTER 4
BASTARDS
I HAVE MET
118

GEORGE JOHNSTON*
JON ZEALANDO*
BRYCE PETERSON
TED AND CHRIS CLARK*
ALEX KING
HELEN RASMUSSEN
GEORGE WILSON

CHAPTER 5
GOLD AND
GREENSTONE
154

BARBARA MAGNER*
CLIFF JOSEPHS*
LLOYD SCOTT*
BOB FIELD*
CRAIG HOWAN*

CHAPTER 6
FROM THE
LETTERBOX
174

CHAPTER 7
WRITINGS
198

*Interviewed by Kirsten Warner

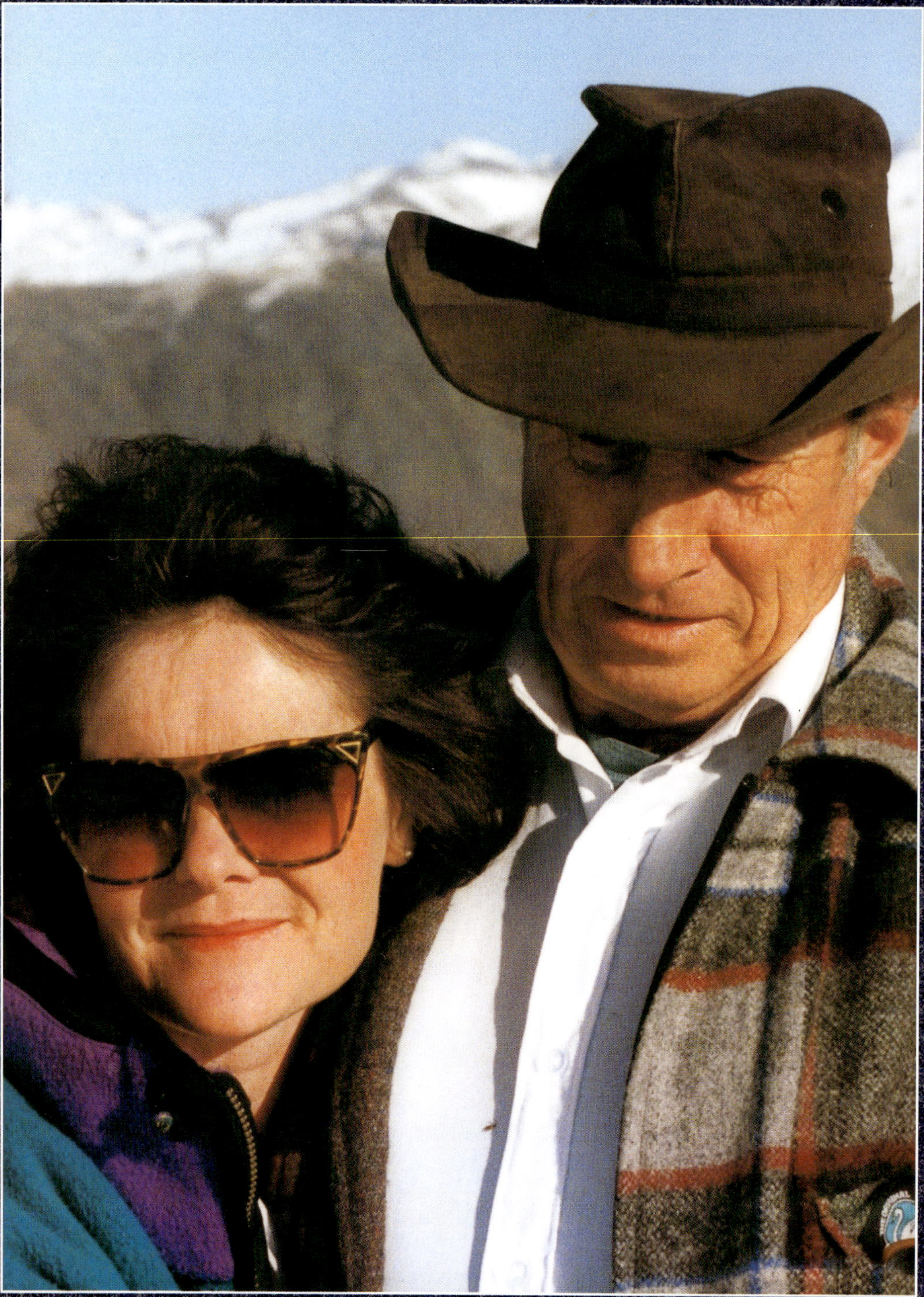

FOREWORD
BY
MAGGIE CRUMP

IN FRONT OF ME I HAVE A STACK OF CRUMPY'S BOOKS, TWENTY-FOUR TITLES IN ALL, REFLECTING FORTY-ODD YEARS OF EXPERIENCES, JOURNEYS, ADVENTURES AND PEOPLE HE MET ALONG THE WAY. MOST OF US NARROW OUR RANGE OF TALES BY making one or two long stops in life and, while the same bus stops, highways, letterboxes and faces may make for security and comfort, these were two luxuries that didn't play a big part in Crumpy's life. He was our great New Zealand wanderer and he suffered all the hardships that a nomadic lifestyle brings with it.

He caught only a glimpse, as he travelled past, of the firelit lounge with the family gathered round.

Crumpy was an enigma. People wanted to know what made this man tick, but just when they thought they had him figured out he would split the scene. He was encumbered with neither possessions nor people. He travelled light – twenty minutes to pack up the Hilux – except for his last departure from Marlborough, which required a furniture removal truck. Perhaps this was the straw that broke the camel's back!

We miss him because he made us laugh. It's the best medicine available without a price tag.

We miss him because he represented simplicity. He wasn't bogged down in materialism. He belonged to an era that was less troubled and more caring.

We miss him because he was humble. He didn't aspire to fame or fortune.

We miss him because he loved the unloved. Most of us aren't that generous.

I miss him because he opened up horizons beyond my imagining and he's not here to share them with me.

All whose paths he crossed will remember him for their own personal encounters. There is no denying the fact that he touched us all.

This book is a dedication from his family and friends. Not by Barry Crump, this time, but for him.

Crumpy was an enigma. People wanted to know what made this man tick, but just when they thought they had him figured out he would split the scene. He was encumbered with neither possessions nor people.

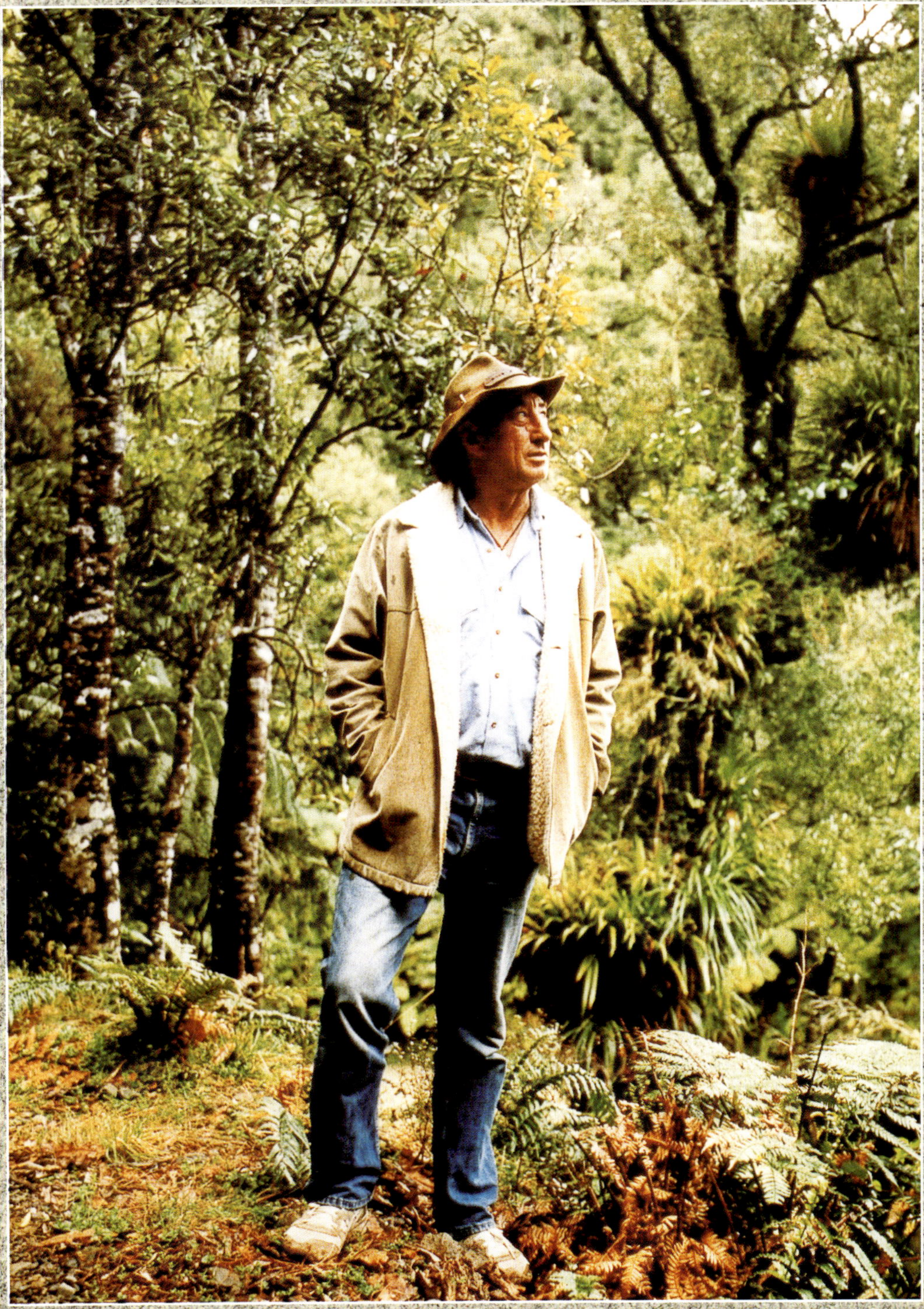

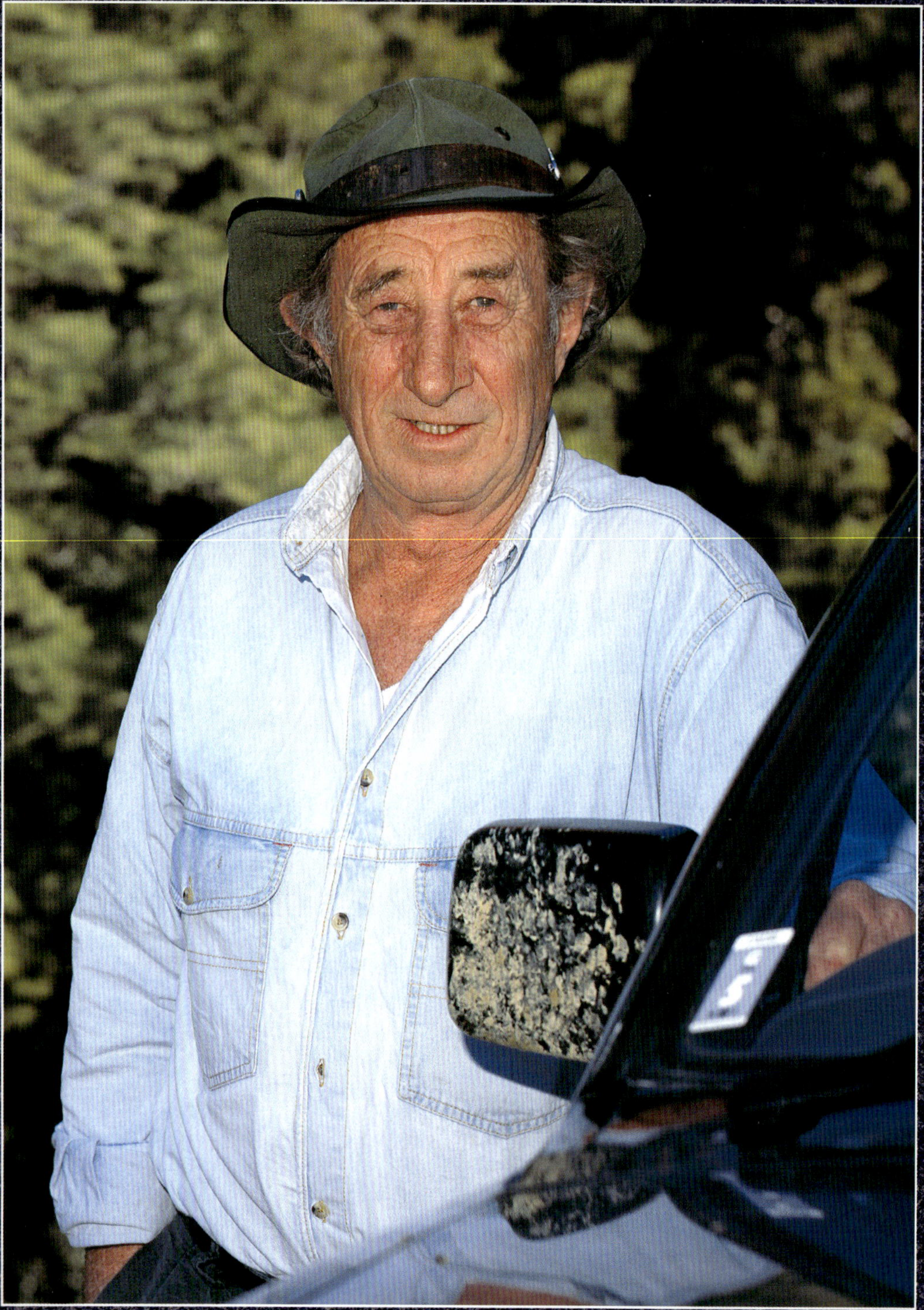

INTRODUCTION
BY
COLIN HOGG

Barry Crump had helped muster 5000 sheep and done a radio interview before he made it down to the pub in Wanaka at noon on a sleepy Friday. "That pig you gave us was good eating," he shouts to a bloke in the bar. "Made a bit of a mess of the back porch when I cut it in half with the chainsaw, though."

He was a hands-on legend, was Crump. And, entrance made on this particular day in the early nineties, he was hands-on to a whisky with an Elephant Beer chaser.

"Look, there's a loopy bus pulling in, cobber," he shouts to the pub manager. The manager was the joker wearing the tie. "You shoulda seen the tie he had on the other day. Looked like he'd vomited," says Crump loudly enough for the manager to hear. "I'll give you five bucks for it."

Crump admitted to having worn a tie a few times (hence the offer). "Some of the things Toyota do, you have to dress up a bit. I don't want to embarrass them." As to the "loopy bus", well that was a bus full of "loopies", Crump's favoured label for tourists. They got a lot of them around Wanaka and Crump tended to not take them seriously. Everyone else tended to make money out of them.

And as for Toyota . . . well, the car company had helped butter the strange bread that was Crump's existence for the previous decade or so. He might have written a daunting number of books and sold an astonishing 1.3 million copies of them, but Crump had hit the end of his fifties probably better known as the laconic star of a series of television ads also featuring his nervous mate 'Scotty' and the Toyota Hilux, a four-wheel-drive Kiwi-joker sort of vehicle that, like Crump, could go anywhere.

Except that Crump probably got there first. He moved around a bit, did Crump. He had, he reckoned, never stayed anywhere more than three months.

"Well, I owned a place for ten years once," he says, "but I never stayed there more than three months. It was the only time I ever left somewhere and had to come back. Bugger that, it's twice the mileage.

"Nah, I'm a groover, I'm a drifter, just like the song says." Crump bursts into a brief basso-profundo rendition of "I was Born Under a Wandering Star".

Wanaka must have been quiet before he arrived.

He'd drifted into town some months before. "I'd lived in this area three years earlier on," he says. "I know the people, I know the stations, the owners. Me and (wife) Maggie were living in the truck with the young guy and the dogs on the West Coast. We drove over the hill one day, over Haast, came in here for a feed, ran into a mate and he said, 'Do you want to rent my house and give us a bit of a hand with the stock?'

"We've been here ever since. The kids are going to school and we're writing great New Zealand novels, aren't we honey potato?" – this last bit to Maggie.

"I just printed out the first chapter of my new book, but I'm not far enough into it to know what the denouement is yet."

Denouement wasn't a word you expected to hear from Crump, but he was full of surprises. At fifty-eight, he had the face of a man who'd never worn sunglasses and if there was a story for every line round his eyes, it seemed he had a lot of books left in him yet.

And if there was any surprise in meeting Barry Crump then it was in the realisation that he was at least as big, in every sense, as the rumours. Standing a solid six feet between his battered old hat and his battered new track shoes, he looked like the sort of bloke you shouldn't mess with, the sort of bloke who might muster 5000 sheep after breakfast and then feel like a bit of a drink.

But he smiled easily and obviously enjoyed a good yarn, decanting the stories, jokes and philosophy in a slow rumble, peppered with the expletives he always deleted from his books.

"I've published a lot of novels and there's not a foul word in them," he says. "I do that here in the pub or in the bedroom. But I can write dialogue that sounds like someone's swearing without using the actual words. Once

"Nah, I'm a groover, I'm a drifter, just like the song says." Crump bursts into a brief basso-profundo rendition of "I was Born Under a Wandering Star".

you start using that sort of language in a novel, you've lowered its tone."

Crump had set his tone way back in 1960 with his first novel, *A Good Keen Man*, a yarn told straight and true from life in the unmistakeable voice of New Zealand. Crump's simple maxim remained, "If it's hard to write, it's hard to read," and it hadn't let him down so far.

A Good Keen Man has sold 300,000 copies – most importantly, many of its buyers have been the sort of Kiwis who'd never normally dream of reading a book. But then at first Crump must have seemed like the sort of Kiwi who wouldn't dream of writing one.

For years he wouldn't even allow himself to be described as a writer. "Bushman" was his label of choice – and it was one he could still argue for. He didn't, though. He was happy now to call himself a writer.

"Well, I am one. I've found a profession I'm good at. It used to be just one of the things I did.

"Most of my life I've kept myself going on possum trapping. Never

"Whenever I move on and have to start up on the road again I get what I privately call my kick-off kit. Tea-bags, a tin of condensed milk, a large tin of peaches and a tin of cream. Cut the tops out of the peach and cream tins and eat the contents. Fold the top of the peach tin into a band and bend it into a handle and wire it into the cream tin. That's me mug. Then I put a wire handle on the peach tin and that's me billy. Then I carve myself a spoon out of a piece of wood and I'm all set up for that best of all drinks, a brew of tea.

– *The Life and Times of a Good Keen Man*

wanted much. Had much, but never wanted it. I own bugger all. I don't even own a set of wheels (the Hilux was on permanent loan)."

All of this, of course, might have seemed a little astonishing for a man who, even if he had earned a couple of bucks for each book sold, should have been a millionaire two or three times over.

"Bloody oath, mate," says Crump. "But I don't want to be like that. I don't think you need that much money. You can only sleep in one bed, you can only eat one feed at a time."

He agreed, though, that there were certain sorts of beds in certain sorts of places and – on a budget scale at least – there were meals and there were feeds.

"Aw yeah, but I've tried all that. Don't want it. I lived in Auckland for six months before I came down here. Right in the middle of town roaming the streets. There are some unloveable creatures come up out of the culverts around one or two in the morning.

"I can handle the big city. A good Kiwi bushman can handle just about everything. Because you've lived it hard, just about everything else is easy by comparison. Sit on one of them ridges up around these parts for a while and see how you can keep yourself warm."

Down the road apiece from the pub, the view from the Crumps' kitchen table seemed custom-made to take a townie's breath away. It was a humble house and I saw what he meant about the pig and the chainsaw – the evidence of the impact was sprayed up the wall by the back door – but inside it was as cosy as outside it wasn't.

The house pointed its back straight down a valley to mountains just waiting to pull the snow right down to their toes. To the right was a row of the giant poplars that mark the landscape so dramatically in Central Otago.

Crump talked movingly of a leaf storm that enveloped the house when a wind lifted the great golden drifts the poplars had deposited. He was a man still helplessly in love with his environment. He'd been full-frontal to it all his life.

He was born in Papatoetoe, the second of what would be a six-pack born to a hard-working, ever-moving sharemilking couple. In his autobiography, *The Life and Times of a Good Keen Man*, he wrote of the Crump kids asking their mother one day how she met the old man.

" 'I was walking along a lane near where we were living and he cantered along on a mare he was breaking in and scooped me up and rode off with me,' she said. And knowing our father that'd be about right."

Barry, one of four boys, was a curious kid in a rugged world that seemed to have more silences than ready answers. "I've always been an ardent searcher, you know," he says, gazing out the window at cloud

slipping across mountain. "When I was a little boy I used to say to people, 'Why are we here?' I'd read jam tim labels looking for the answer. I'd hear an uncle was coming I hadn't met and I'd think, 'Oh he might know,' and I'd go up to him and say, 'Uncle Tim, why are we here?'

"And he'd say, 'C'mon Barry, go outside and play with the other kids'. A new teacher might come. I'd asked all the others and they were already highly suspicious of me. First thing, the bell rang and I ran up and said, 'Why are we here?'

" 'Go and sit down at once,' she said. And I thought, 'She doesn't know either.' "

This wasn't the sort of thing you expected to hear falling out of Crump's worn and famous face. It didn't quite fit with the man who, if you read a lot of his books, had done his level best to level the population of pigs, possums, rabbits and deer all over New Zealand – not to mention crocodile in the far north of Australia.

But what might have seemed like conflicting emotions in someone else fitted strangely together in Crump. The man's spirituality stretched way beyond the whisky in his hand. To stay true he'd had to stay outside and, in staying outside, he'd come to realise he'd never fitted in anyway.

"I knew I didn't belong here when I was about three," he says, leaning forward, sharing a secret. "I don't belong here. I'm willing to fit into any niche, put my heart and soul into anything I've ever belonged to and I've come to the conclusion that I was dead right when I was three."

Crump grew up believing in radio serials and Jack London's *Call of the Wild*. In *The Life and Times of a Good Keen Man* he wrote, "I spent a fair bit of time in a world I made up for myself. They used to call me 'Dopey' because I was always away with the fairies."

At the age of eight, aside from dreaming, he was trapping rabbits with his father, turning solo to trap possum. Growing up, he worked as a farmhand, spending most of his wages on ammunition, hunting. He moved around, his dogs for company, breaking horses, fencing, scrub-cutting, tractor driving, deer culling, hunting, always open to experience.

He got married, became a father, moved to Auckland, worked on building sites, drove trucks, dealt to the possum population of the Waitakeres. He met new wildlife, falling in with the arty, literary crowd, read Thurber and Huxley, Nancy Mitford and Banjo Paterson and was talked into writing a short story for a literary magazine.

He was surprised at how easy it was, at how much he enjoyed it. The marriage ended – as another three would in Crump's life – but a book started soon after. He turned out *A Good Keen Man* in a month and, by the time it was published and starting to make him famous, he was back

I've actually done the things I read about and dreamed of doing when I was a boy on the farm. I've climbed the mountains and hunted the deer and the boar. I've lived in the bush and run traplines for my living, and been in blizzards and floods. I've harpooned the big saurian from the prow of my little boat. I know what it's like to be shipwrecked and nearly die of thirst, and to be marooned on a tropical island. I've travelled through strange lands and lived with people on the other side of the world. I've paddled canoes through steaming tropical jungles and dived in a coral lagoon and ridden a giant turtle out across a reef. It's a bit strange to think I did all that and then wrote it down without realising it was the fulfilment of vivid childhood dreams.

I don't know how much I've changed during all this, but I do notice that the hand that once drove the harpoon into the neck of a big saltwater crocodile, now reaches down to pluck aside a worm before I ram my posthole.

– The Life and Times of a Good Keen Man

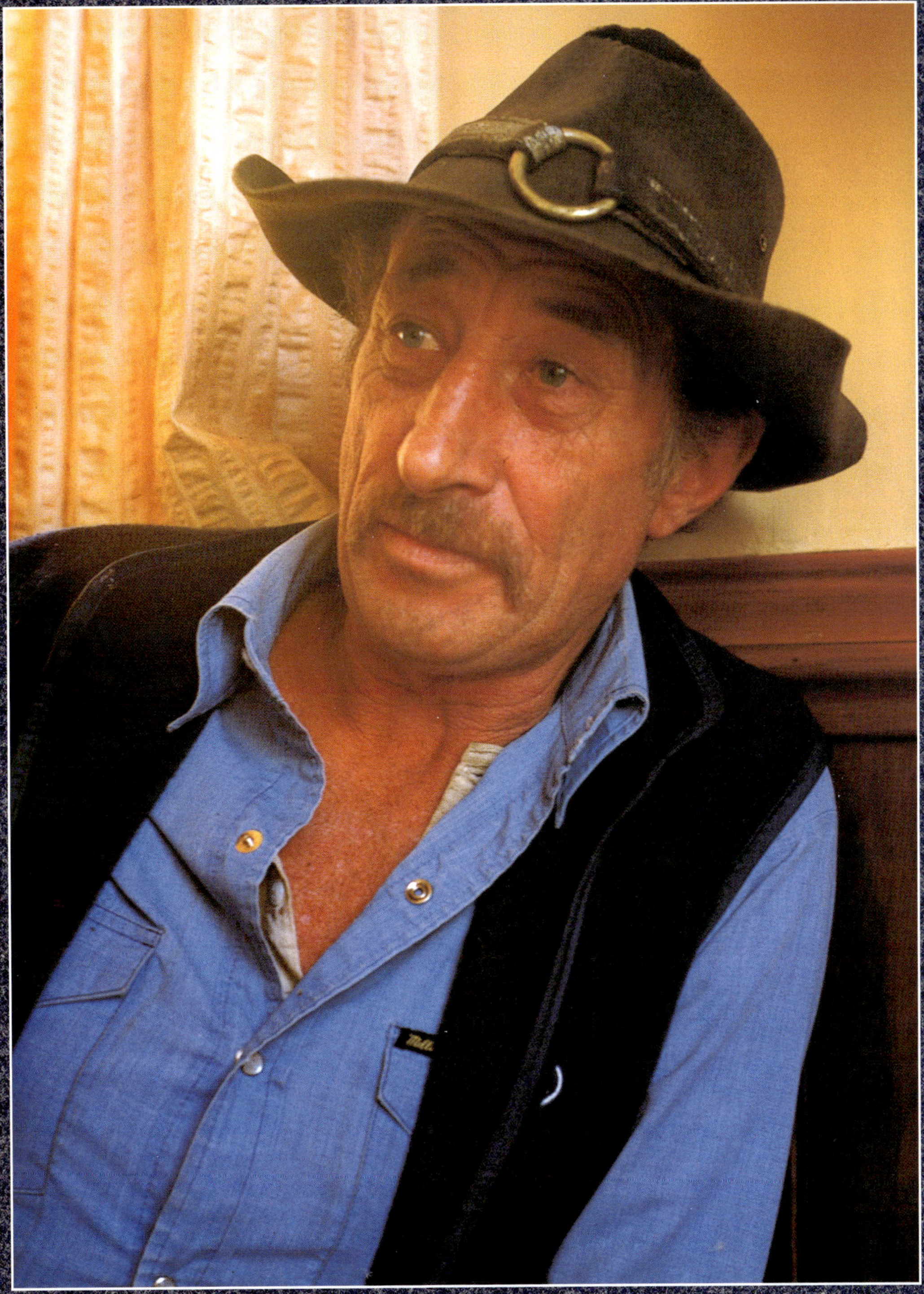

in the bush, rabitting.

And ever since, the living and the writing have been virtually inseparable.

"When I'm writing, I live it," he says. "Like for *Gold and Greenstone*, I went and lived it all again. That'll come through to the reader. It's very easy to go to the Alexander Turnbull Library, you know, and look up all sorts of things – documents, letters, records . . . And some of them do that.

"I don't. I go out and do it again. And that, I think, is what's refreshing. It's also hard work."

The writing, he reckoned, came easy. "I like doing it. I love it. If it's hard, I don't do it. I just stop. If it's hard to write, it's going to be hard to read.

"I've got a formula for starting. I write a whole lot of nonsense. I just decide I'm going to write a book and sit down and start writing whatever seems important at that moment. And before you've gone half a page, you're away . . . It's a tricky business, eh? People tell me they could write a book and I look at them and say, 'I don't think you could'.

"You need a sustained amount of autobiography."

Crump had that – along with the aforementioned sustained amount of income, as a result of the books that kept on coming and the readers who queued up to make him New Zealand's best-selling author.

"I've been rich," says Crump. "I've had that much money I haven't known what to do with it. All I do is get drunk and make a fool of myself somewhere."

There was the occasional more inspired moment, though.

"I remember one day waiting for a taxi in Wellington and a whole lot of other people were waiting round. Some of them were in a bit more of a hurry than me. It was a taxi rank right opposite Wellington Motors and after a while I got fed up with waiting too and went over and bought a car off the guy.

"The funny thing about that was I had a ticket on a plane to Queensland in two days. I lost 700 quid on that car. That was a lot of money back in the sixties," says Crump wistfully. He'd never, he said, quite managed to just lie back and enjoy his gains.

"It's not being able to," he says. "My friends have said to me many many times, 'You could be rich, you could be associating with the most influential and wonderful people'. Well, I'm still here. I've followed my heart. Don Clark was kicking goals with his bare feet when I was a household word as well as him.

"It was no great intellectual ability of mine. It was just following me heart. As for writing, I found I could get through to people. I feel as if I've been worthwhile. Whereas if I'd taken advantage of it or let somebody take me over, I don't think I could feel as pleased about my life as I feel right now.

"I remember as a young boy hearing a neighbour remarking to another neighbour, 'If them Crump boys survive to grow up, they'll be tough'. I didn't understand that until later. Looking back on our old man, he was a hard bastard – a good one, but a hard one. And as it turns out there is a strong brotherhood between us three oldest boys – Brother Bill, Brother Barry and Brother Colin. Friends have tried in vain to get in between us.

"My younger brother Colin, he's always been a wonderful man. He was a millionaire when there were only about six in the country. And my older brother has never had two bob to rub together, but a magic person, eh? I love him for the same reason his mates do.

"He's a ranger, brother Bill, in the Tasman Park. Done heaps. In fact, a lot of the things brother Bill talks to me about, I write about. He's got a wonderful spirit. Very nice man. I'm proud of him.

"The writing scene in this country has deteriorated along with everything else. But there are things people like. They like to read something that makes them laugh. But there's no humour in New Zealand literature at the moment."

"We are proud of each other, us brothers. We all went through the same heavy stuff in the first place in our lives."

Crump didn't suffer fools gladly. Wife Maggie, summing up life with him, said, "He's hard to live with and he's lovely to live with. He's good. He knows he's good and other people aren't always up to his expectations."

The people of the book world apparently hadn't been. "A great wad of wankers" is how Crump gently described those people who stood between him and his audience. "Mr Greedy stands between me and the reader. Some of the book shops demand sixty percent, to cover their backsides.

"People don't read much any more anyway. I'd rather watch telly than read a novel."

Really?

"Not really, but yeah. Mostly through laziness. The writing scene in this country has deteriorated along with everything else. But there are things people like. They like to read something that makes them laugh. But there's no humour in New Zealand literature at the moment."

Which was hardly surprising, according to Crump, given the state of the national mood.

"I go from the north to the south of this land. I'm in touch with what they're saying everywhere and I've never seen this country so united since World War Two. You can walk into any bar in this land and say, 'Aren't they a pack of losers?' and you'll get agreement from everybody in the bar – Labour or National or whatever.

"But what we're laughing with these days is a cynical laughter that I can't use in books. We're laughing at our bureaucrats and the bureaucrats are all looking after their own alley, scared for their jobs and they can't even do those properly.

"If you or I did a job like they do, we'd be out of it straight away. And here we are confronted by these people. They're gone, man, they're finished," says Crump. "Our bureaucracy will crumble and disintegrate through its own inefficiency and a total lack of understanding of the situation.

"Fancy putting people on the dole. All the political parties agreed on that – stick 'em on the dole. If you want to bring a society undone without firing a shot, just pay the young people not to do anything.

"Our politicians are displaying a profound ignorance of human nature. That's why we've got all sorts of terrible things going on in this land. And I'm trying to write humour?

"We're surrounded by exploded theories and the huge money-wasting of the tax-gatherers. The media's the same. No one cares about the people.

"I care. I really care about the people. When I write a book, I'm writing it to my best mate, someone I really love."

Though, passing on 1.3 million love letters could make life a little crowded. With the aid of those Toyota ads, only a 'loopy' could have failed to recognise Crump.

"By them I subsist," he says. "They give me the freedom to travel the roads. They buy my books. The fame part has faded into the background. What it resolves itself into is handling people in the pubs, in the streets, the milkbars.

"They all know me, they all say the same thing by way of intro, 'What happened to Scotty?' or, 'How did you get that truck up the cliff?' Mostly to do with the Toyota ads."

Even the birth of the ads had been written into the Crump myth.

"I was living in a Model A that I'd rebuilt, but it was causing too many near-accidents," he explains. "It would only do about fifty kilometres, otherwise it would overheat, start steaming and carrying on. We lived in that for about four years and it crapped out.

"I'd fixed everything. We couldn't get a warrant of fitness. We were living on a golf course – Waitakere Golf Course, actually – and we were going down Lincoln Road in Henderson and I saw a Toyota four-wheel-drive, the first one I'd seen. I got onto the guy in charge and said, 'I'll advertise them if you give me one.

"That was ten or twelve years ago. They employed me and Scotty to do the ads and we've been mates ever since. Laurel and Hardy, eh? A bit of humour."

Crump didn't have any trouble dealing with the advertising world. "I'm very straight, eh? I said, 'You pay me that and I'll do this' – and they do."

For a straight man, though, Crump often seemed downright evasive in his autobiography, a yarn that was grand on the grand scale, but notably short on personal stuff.

"I am an evasive person," says Crump. "I don't want no trouble from anybody. I'm weaving my way through it and I'm keeping my strides on and my head down. And if you stick your head up, they will take a shot at you and you'll be caught in a withering crossfire . . .

"In my autobiography there's no dirty washing. I know I could have sold a lot of books if I'd revealed something about someone or exposed something. But I'm proud of the fact that no one can find any dirty washing in my writing or what I do or say or what I am."

Crump the philosopher was a strange mix of liberal and rugged individual. "I know lots of people in this world and if I ever get in trouble in a strange town, I'll go to a gay guy or a butch chick or a prostitute or one of us low bastards and say, 'Hey give us a hand, I'm a bit stuffed,' and I'll get help."

Whereas, he said, if he went to the so-called pillars of society, "they wouldn't want to know about you.

"Where do you go? I go by heart," he says. "That way, I've never gone wrong. It's scary. It scares the living daylights out of you.

"And when you're driving with no bread, you've got a dog for a mate and you're going into a strange town wondering if there's a gas station open and lightning glimpse into the livingroom of some suburban house, you think, 'What the hell am I doing out here?'

"So I've given in and set up with my darling. But at least I know the other side and I appreciate this. If you can't appreciate what you've got, you'll never be able to appreciate anything."

He remained something of the ultimate lonely guy, all the same.

"I have a detachment. There's no way a detached person can get attached. It's got its agonies . . . loneliness is the worst part of it and loneliness is all it's cracked up to be, mate.

"Sometimes when I'm lonely, I feel best. I've been deer culling, fifteen miles away from the nearest human being. Now, that's detached, but that's suitable for the occasion, if you know what I mean.

"The other detachment is being apart, looking in on things, seeing things with a clear eye because you're not in there."

Crump had found his personal answers in his faith – Baha'i, a non-confrontational religion whose tenets include a laudable reluctance to proselytise or, as Crump put it, "We don't punish anyone's lug with it. It's not conducive to giving them knowledge and understanding of what this is all about."

The boy who read jam tin labels looking for an answer reckoned he'd found it. "I searched and I know I'm responsible and I know that this is the truth. And I know that the apples on the tree don't all ripen at the same time. We've all got to go through a certain amount of trouble, but I see myself in the ditch, legging up some of the ones who aren't so well off as me.

"And I'm pleased that I am like that. I've discovered in this life that you can do anything you like so long as you don't muck somebody else up. I know I haven't written a full autobiography – maybe someone else will – but I've always been careful not to be seen blowing my own trumpet. I don't like arrogance in people."

And, he said, the thing that reassured him he was on the right track was the number of people who said the first book they ever managed to read was one of his. "People handling dyslexics or difficult-to-teach kids have written me letters that are thoroughly heart-warming. More heart-warming than hearing you've sold 20,000 copies."

For all the heart-warming he did, he still stopped a lot of animals' ones.

"I don't kill anything I don't want. But on the other hand I don't want to be like one of those Indians who goes round scrubbing the ground with a branch in case he treads on an ant. I don't like killing anything. The enjoyment was never in destroying the animal. I wrote once, 'If you're starting enjoying cutting throats there's something bad wrong with you'."

He said that was a macho hang-over from the day when the best hunter was the best provider among "us young men".

"That's fading now. At least we had that. Rightly or wrongly, we felt that was worth doing. Now our young men can't think of anything worth doing."

Crump never had any such problems. On paper, in the flesh or in the popular mythology of New Zealand, he had a personality so big you'd have to put boots on to walk around in it. And a strong sense of himself.

"I'm better person to person . . . off the cuff. Yeah, they don't forget me off the cuff."

He wasn't kidding. Shirts had been known to shrink in his presence.

"We're surrounded by exploded theories and the huge money-wasting of the tax-gatherers. The media's the same. No one cares about the people.

"I care. I really care about the people. When I write a book, I'm writing it to my best mate, someone I really love."

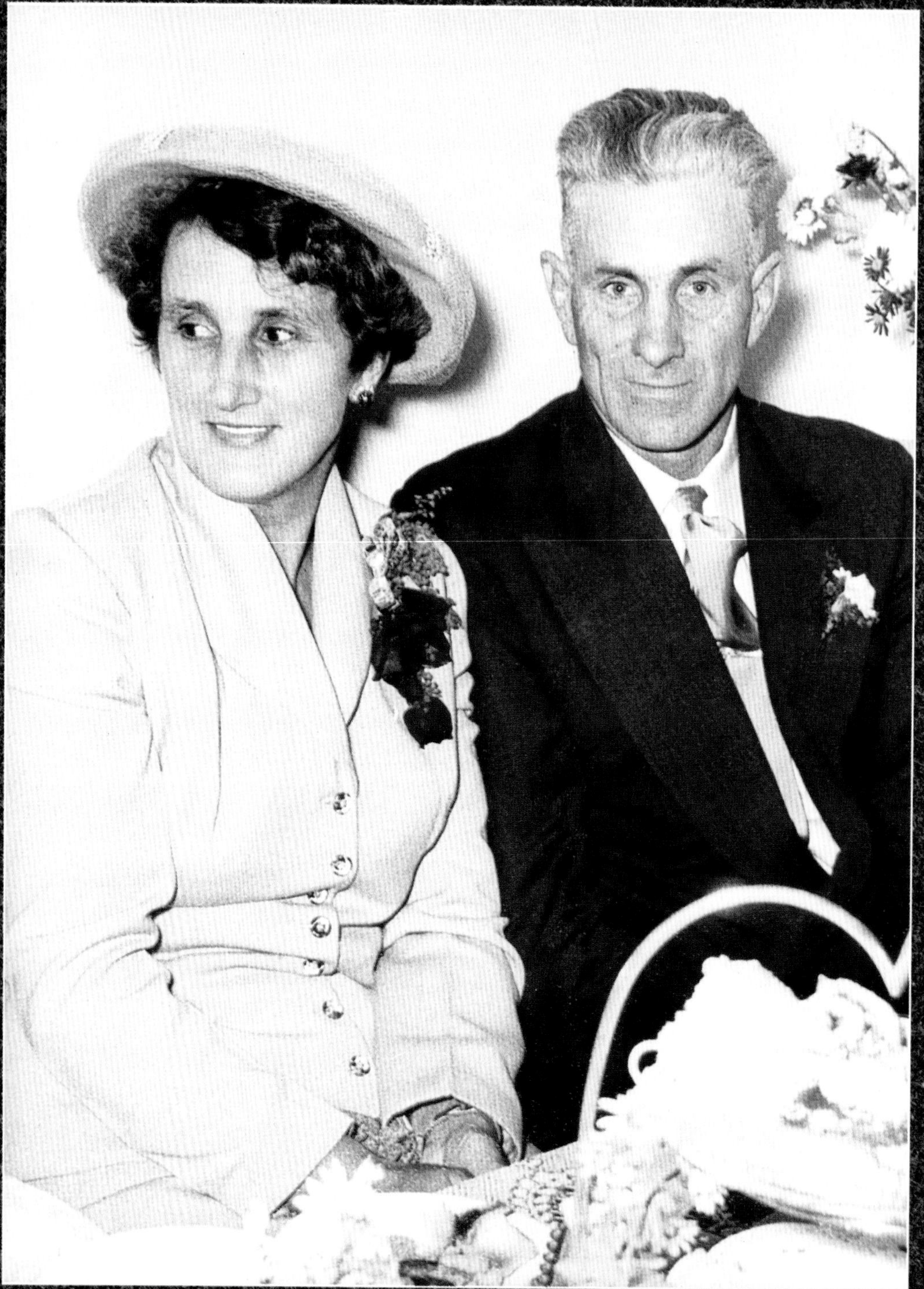

Chapter 1
ONE OF US

The milkings were always the same. The pulsing suction of the milking-machines, the whine of the cream-separator, the bawling of calves and the clang of cream-cans on the wet concrete. The squealing of the pigs as they clamoured at the white cascades of skim-dick being poured into their troughs. Then up to the house, fresh cream on our porridge and off to school. Don't be late home for the milking, and no picking the bread on the way up from the gate or you might cop a 'reek under the lug' from the old man. Being dealt to by our father could be quite dramatic, but a clout with the copper-stick from Mum was a joke, bless her.

– The Life and Times of a Good Keen Man

BILL CRUMP
(Barry's older brother)

W E Crump men all move around a lot. We love it. I think we got that in our early days because we went to so many schools. We used to change places every year because our father was in great demand. Someone would always offer more money for the next season and we'd be on our way. We were just leaping and bounding from one place to another. I don't know, we may have picked up a bug in those days.

The old man accumulated bugger all. He was a shocking gambler. He'd crawl through twenty feet of snow to put ten bob each way on a horse if he knew there was a bloody meeting on. That's where all the money went, the bit he did get.

Our father was quite a violent person. I don't know what in a man's nature would make him so bitter, so that not only would he do terrible things but he would never, ever show any remorse about it. It was something that no one could put a finger on. He was pretty brilliant at some things too – he played a beautiful hand on piano, he read music, he was one of the best blacksmiths around and an excellent farmer. He was highly respected by everyone in the area as one of the best in all-round farming technique, although it was just bloody hard work really. He didn't treat anybody kindly, though, not any living thing.

Barry and I got most of the beatings, and we used to spend great lengths of time planning our father's death. We were fair dinkum about it. But what a terrible thing for teenagers to be doing. The last incident before

I left home was when he'd been giving my sister a bad time and I just warned him, if he ever did that again I'd do him in. I think he could have killed me at that instant but he chose not to, that's all.

I know that there were good times, but we were so overwhelmed by the bad things that we've just switched ourselves off and we can't remember. There's eight years of my life I can't remember. I know I was there, I know I went to school, but that's all.

The Brotherhood . . . Brother Bill, Brother Barry, Brother Colin: "We were just leaping and bounding from one place to another. I don't know, we may have picked up a bug in those days."

I think these incidents, these family problems, just brought Mum and us kids closer together in the long run. Our sister Carol doesn't remember too much of the violence because she was that much younger and she missed out, thank goodness, and young Peter would never have known what it was. By the time they came along the old man's violence had tapered right off. He'd got away from the farm scene and, from what I heard, although I was away for years at a time, he was somewhat mellowed. Then Mum and him split up and we never had to have anything more to do with the rugged side of things.

I've got my father's flare, a quick temper, but I'm not violent, no bloody way. Cruelty to people and animals just doesn't make sense. I'm sure it was something my father had no control over. I don't think in the long run he ever felt proud of it. He never said sorry, but he was pig-headed, stubborn, and any show of compassion might have been regarded as a weakness.

It surprised me when Barry turned out to be a writer. Barry never had a clue about things, he was pretty dumb at school. I never thought he'd get on anywhere. We were going to Otahuhu College and I didn't handle it too badly, but Barry didn't like school to a bad degree. He could be plain naughty. They'd tell him, "Pull your socks up, put your cap on," and he'd stick his cap in his back pocket and go sauntering past them with his socks down around his ankles.

He did go home once feeling pretty sore and he broke down a bit. When he was trying to mumble to Mum what the trouble was, the old man said, "What the hell's wrong with you?"

"Oh, teacher gave me six straps on the back and it's still hurting," said Barry. And the old man just dragged him off and gave him six more. He reckoned no teacher knows how to flog a man properly. You'd never talk back to the old man.

As soon as I turned fifteen I left Otahuhu College and started working at the wharf to get the money to shift out. In those days, once you'd learned everything the school had to teach you the world was your oyster and you had to get out there and make yourself available to it. So you had to move on. I didn't see my mother for eight years, one part of it. We were close, but that didn't make any difference. We really were remorseless about leaving. We just turned our back on home and went out.

After we left home, Barry took off into the bush hunting for Internal Affairs, and I didn't see him for about four years until he came and found me in Atiamuri. He got a job for the Department of Lands and Survey in the woolshed down the road a bit, and ended up rabbiting over near the Mihi Bridge on the Rotorua-Taupo road. But even when I knew he wasn't that far down the road I didn't necessarily get to see him very often.

It must have been 1963 when Barry came to where I was working in Putaruru. Every time Barry turned up he had a big truckload of grog, so we all had to knock off until it was gone. It used to upset my boss but at least it didn't happen too often. We had a nice big reception area where we used to do our celebrating, we used to call it the fornicatorium. We weren't interfering with any home scene; we preferred it that way.

I hadn't seen Barry for a couple of years and I didn't know where he'd been. Barry was telling us about his experiences in Australia, crocodile hunting and all that sort of thing, and then he asked me why didn't I go back with him. "Not a problem," I told him. "Just wait a minute until I grab me boots and I'll join you," and we hopped on the plane and took off back there. Well, I didn't get back to New Zealand until 1974. I had seven kids and I had to turn my back on all that. My marriage had been on the rocks for a long time. I had been under a fair old strain for quite a while and the kids needed their mother, so I thought the best thing I could do was get the hell out of there and send money home.

Without trying to, we just took over Cooktown. It sounds an incredibly broad thing to say, but that's how it turned out. There were only 300 people there, with three hotels. It was a very, very country place, 200 kilometres north of Cairns and the road was not even worth thinking about. The place

Cooktown was the first Australian town I'd really got to know, and what a crazy, wonderful frontier-type place it was in those days.
— The Life and Times of a Good Keen Man

had a degree of isolation which was really wonderful. It set up a society which was just an absolute joy to have anything to do with. And of course the Brotherhood began there.

We've always called ourselves Brother Bill, Brother Barry, and soon the whole town was doing the same. Even our bank statements were Brother Bill, Brother Barry, and our mail. The whole town joined in.

"Whose shout is it?"

"Oh, it's Brother George's." Even the publican wanted to be called Brother.

Every time I see any one of the Aussies they say, "Gidday, Brother Bill, how's Brother Barry?" and they're looking over my shoulder for him. They've never given up hoping to see him again. He made a tremendous impression around Cairns and wherever he was.

His companion Jean Watson (pictured with Crumpy and me right) was with him then, although they split up for a time and she signed on as a jillaroo. She was an amazing person and she has never told anyone one-tenth of the things she was involved in over there.

We shot crocs in a sixteen-foot clinker-built with spotlighting. One night out hunting, we had a croc on board, only about fourteen feet long – not a big one. We'd chopped it through the back of the neck, so it was definitely dead, but they have a death reflex and when it whipped its jaws open and went bang, Jeannie thought it had come to. She was working the outboard motor at the back and she threw herself straight over backwards. She couldn't swim – she's never swum, she just floats around – but we left her there while we had a quick look round the corner up front in case there was a good one lurking there. It did look a bit bad, but Brother Barry reckoned, no, leave her there. We told her not to make a bloody noise when we were spotlighting. We found her later, she was always a survivor.

Even when she's telling the story she's got the wonderful gaiety of a child of six or seven who enjoyed bathing in crocodile-infested waters. I asked her at Barry's funeral why she's never told people about all her marvellous adventures. "Oh, you think I should?" she said in her dainty little old way. She doesn't tell the story with the enthusiasm that it deserves, but she's been there – my God, has she ever.

We three were very close – she was actually looking after me as well as Barry. Poor Jeannie was working her guts out. She was only quite a scrawny woman and yet she had wonderful powers of resistance. She's been with us in very tricky situations at times.

Of course, we got shipwrecked too. That was embarrassing. We were taking paying passengers out to the Great Barrier Reef. One of the passengers was a retired bloody police superintendent from Melbourne, and he was the cause of the whole bloody problem.

It was very difficult to anchor a boat in that water, and we were keeping an eye on it. I saw the mast moving and I thought I'd better get out there and let some rope out, but the superintendent had pinched the dinghy to go back on board to get a shirt. In that time the boat had drifted off from the shallow water and into the deep with this idiot on board. He just hung on to it until she drifted onto the beach on the mainland about eighteen kilometres away.

We had a terrible thirty-six hours, I can tell you. No shelter, no water, nothing. It wasn't nice. We never wore much gear when we were sailing – it was the tropics – and so the midday sun burned the hell out of us. Another twenty-four hours would have done for us. We were very, very lucky to get

picked up off the coral – it was miles from anywhere – but a New Zealand yacht spotted us.

About two years after we got to Australia, we left Barry on Lizard Island at his request. He had a book to finish and the arrangement was we'd join him about three weeks later or whenever. Not long after we left he got picked up, and we heard on the radio and from the police he'd been taken to Port Moresby as an internationally distressed person. The boat took him off to Papua New Guinea and then he was obliged to go back to New Zealand. I didn't see Barry again for about five years, I think.

Australia was the only place Barry and I spent a long time in close contact. After that Barry and I would have a week at a time getting together and catching up on the news. In about 1984 he and Robyn spent six months or so in Golden Bay, where I was living, while my wife Sigrid and I were in Europe. He more or less took over the place while I was away, but as soon

" 'You're sure you know what you're doing, Shirl? If you don't open the door I'm coming in just the same.'

"She slammed the window, yelling for him to wait till he was sober.

"Tony walked across to his truck, got a chainsaw off the back and started her up. Sounded like a full-grown motor-bike race. Then he went up and shoved her fair through the wall of his flash new Government-loan house. He ripped her down one side, across the top, down the other side and along the bottom. There was smoke and sparks and sawdust and noise all over the place. Never seen so much damage done so quickly in all me life. He carved a hole you could have driven this truck through and booted the whole section into his lounge with the carpets and pictures on the walls."

– Hang on a Minute Mate

as I got back he took off. It was embarrassing for him: everywhere he went people wanted to talk to him about his books and all he wanted to do was talk to me. He was constantly harassed and he'd be constantly apologising to me about it.

When he published the first book I didn't think anything terribly special about it but once he became famous I was a bit overawed by it all. When he came back from Australia that time I remember he was writing *Gulf* for Reeds and they had a mighty argument because they said he had to kill off the hero and Barry wasn't having anything of it. Anyway they settled on the hero choking to death on a bottle top he'd taken off a beer bottle with his teeth. One of my tricks.

Barry did actually use some of my experiences for some of his books, not that I minded. They were just stories. Like the one in *Hang on a Minute Mate* he took from when I used the chainsaw to get into the house. I didn't think anyone else should copy me, but it wasn't such a big deal for me – the wife wasn't letting me in and I just wanted to teach her a lesson.

I remember when we took off for Australia and old A. H. Reed drove me separately from Barry out to the airport and just begged me to make sure that Barry got on with the next book because they wanted to get it out for Father's Day. He pleaded with me, "Just make sure he finishes the bloody thing, will you?" And at the airport he turned to me and he said, "Look, Bill, if you ever put pen to paper, I guarantee to print the bugger for you too."

Cooktown... two hundred miles from the nearest other town, Cairns, over a road that was frequently closed in the dry season and always closed in the wet. Most of the freight and passengers came and went on the Malands, a hundred-foot boat that called in every two or three weeks. The population was mostly made up of people from all over who'd called in for the weekend and couldn't get away from the place, and they were as colourful as the place itself, the climate and the coast, the river and the reef, the history and the wildlife and the sheer abundance that was Cooktown in the fifties and sixties.

There was Rum Jungle Jim McKenzie; accidentally blew one of his trocus-shell diver's brains out with a rusty .44 rifle trying to scare away sharks when he was skippering a pearling-lugger in the Timor Sea, and he'd pensioned himself off in Cooktown, energetically blotting out the memory of floating brains and steaming blood with large shots of schnapps and beer chasers in Jimmy Adamson's pub, recounting experiences around the coasts and islands of North Australia that made me feel I was born too late for real adventure, dropping it on me for the loan of a quid until pension day before staggering off into the dark, still chuckling at his own last joke, to be beaten up by a wallaby he surprised in the porch of his shack down by the river.

→ The Life and Times of a Good Keen Man

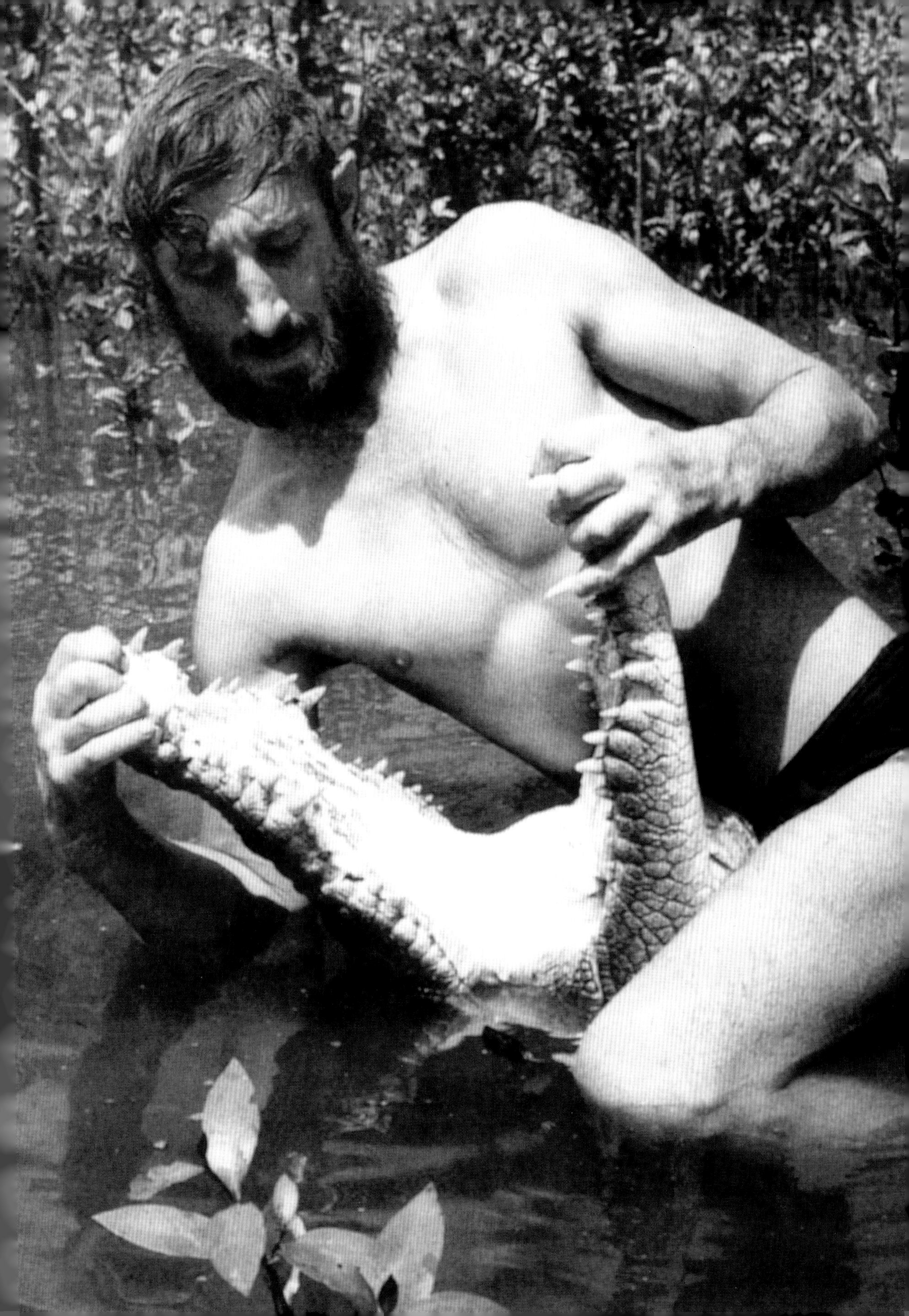

COLIN CRUMP
(Barry's younger brother)

I remember the very first example of Barry's cleverness with words and his first bit of writing. We were both in the same class at Hobsonville School, and we were given the title 'Whip Behind' and told to write an essay. It was a pretty funny title and a bit difficult to form any kind of story about, especially when you're only about ten or eleven years old.

Barry built his story around an olden-days coach and coachman and the 'whip behind' phrase came in with someone calling out to the coachman to use his whip on a guy trying to hitch a free ride on the back. It was a very good story and I remember the teachers buzzing about it and showing it to one another. Nobody else's story was even looked at, Barry's was so well done.

Our Mum, Lily Valley Hendery, was a great story teller. She was a lovely woman, and very gifted and intelligent. She was born in Winiata, near Taihape. I remember my mother's mother, Alice Hendery. Barry was born in her bedroom in the family home at Papatoetoe when the rest of the Hendery family settled there, and Mum and Dad lived with them for a while. Mother's family was poor but respectable. In the early days her father's family had pioneered a big farm on the slopes of Pirongia but because of inexperience had run into financial trouble and sold the farm.

My mum was deeply religious – Apostolic or Assembly of God – pretty charismatic. Her brother Eric was also very religious. He was a pastor in the Apostolic Church, a very gentle man who worked as a radio technician. Her mother used to talk in tongues, not just in church but also in her own home. We used to hear her and think it was very strange. Grandma Hendery was a lovely painter, and specialised in paintings of Christ. Mum used to paint too.

When our parents met, Mum's family were living on a farm at Paparimu, near Hunua. The Crumps were on a neighbouring farm and Wally, the eldest son, took a shine to my mother Lily. Wally's father was a farmer and a blacksmith and our old man worked as a blacksmith too. There were some things the old man was quite good at, for example he was a good shot with a rifle and he could jump his own height at forty years old. But everything he ever did which was half decent was shadowed by a horrible cloud of violence.

My father's mother Annie came out to New Zealand from Scotland with her family and lived at Bombay. She was a lovely person, Grandma Crump, and a real lady. My father's father was William Robert Crump; he was in the cavalry during the First World War and got a bullet wound in the neck. He was a lay preacher in the Methodist Church.

Our father worked as a sharemilker on different farms and as kids Barry and I went to twelve schools. The old man's name was Walter William Crump but everyone called him Wally. He never, ever called us by our names and we never, ever called him Dad. We called him the old man. In later years I called him Wally. That was about the extent of our relationship.

Mum was a lovely, hardworking woman, we all loved her so and he treated her miserably. She was brilliant with a sewing machine. In later years she actually taught night-school sewing and at the Singer Sewing Machine Company in Otahuhu. Mum would get bundles and bundles of old clothes, cut them up, and make them into the most fantastic kids' clothes. The old man would take them up north and sell them.

People want to know why Barry was so restless, always moving on, and why he never was a father to any of his kids. It runs in the family. At Barry's funeral one of my uncles met one of his sons who he hadn't seen for more than forty years. Then at my father's funeral a few weeks later, the same uncle met his other son for the first time in over forty years.

Barry and I were in the cowshed by the time we were five. We milked eighty cows in a six-plant shed morning and night, mostly with the old man but sometimes by the time we were seven and eight we'd do it on our own.

We were always in bare feet, and it was freezing bloody cold at 4 am. We used to look for fresh cow dung to stand in for a minute or two to warm our feet.

Barry and I always had the fondest memories for the times we had together as kids. We went up rivers, we built huts, we fished, we hunted, we trapped hawks and possums and stoats and weasels. We had some wonderful times, but always they were very short-lived because we had to go back to the milking shed and face the old man.

Barry wouldn't talk to people about the old man. He'd say, "Oh yeah, he was pretty rough on us," but he would never use his background to justify anything. We spoke together a bit, but that's where it finished – he wouldn't talk to anyone else about it. He spoke to me about it because we shared it.

As soon as I was fifteen (slightly before, actually) I quit school and cycled off with a bit of gear in a sack to a job on a dairy farm a few miles south of Auckland. I was out on my own. I'd been looking forward to this for years.

– *The Life and Times of a Good Keen Man*

Brother Barry

For fancy cars and city life
He cared not much for these
He'd rather be in river beds
And camp sites in the trees.
Down mountain streams and craggy trails
He'd stalk across the land
In search of deer and pigs or goats,
Yeah – he's a 'Good Keen Man'

He never ever cast a vote
He couldn't figure them out
They're too removed from nature
And what it's all about
He hated war and loss of life
He cared about us all
And nature was his guiding light
The wilderness was his call.

A sleeping bag and rifle
And a swandri on his back
And strapped across his shoulders
Just the usual hunter's pack
Well worn boots and a leather hat
And trusty knife at hand
Not much else was needed
By this really 'Good Keen Man'

His favourite horse
And a dog called Blue
Were part of Crumpy's scene
And so was Scottie and a Toyota ute'
That they crashed into a stream
Scores of books and Tele ads
And even a M.B.E.
He achieved so much in so little time
This man they called 'Crumpy'.

He could ram in a post
And string a fence true
He could plough with a six horse team.
He was one of the few that everyone knew
That survived where we'd never been
And late in the night
When his typewriter rang
If you called him for tea 'cause it's late
I can still hear him say
In his own special way
"Yeah – just hang on a minute, Mate".

A thousand yarns on,
In the pubs and the bars
His stories in books or in song
We laughed and listened to every damn one,
Some were a half mile long.
He told a tale well
Like nobody can
And there's those that will never forget
Of the Life and the Times of
a 'Good Keen Man'
And the bastards that he met

But now Barry's gone
Yet his spirit lives on
Out there somewhere in the trees
With possums and deer
And the birds of the bush
Enduring the wintery freeze.
And if you're ever there
Near a creek or a trail
Just stop and listen and wait
And you'll hear him say
in his own special way
"Hang on a minute, Mate."

By Colin Crump

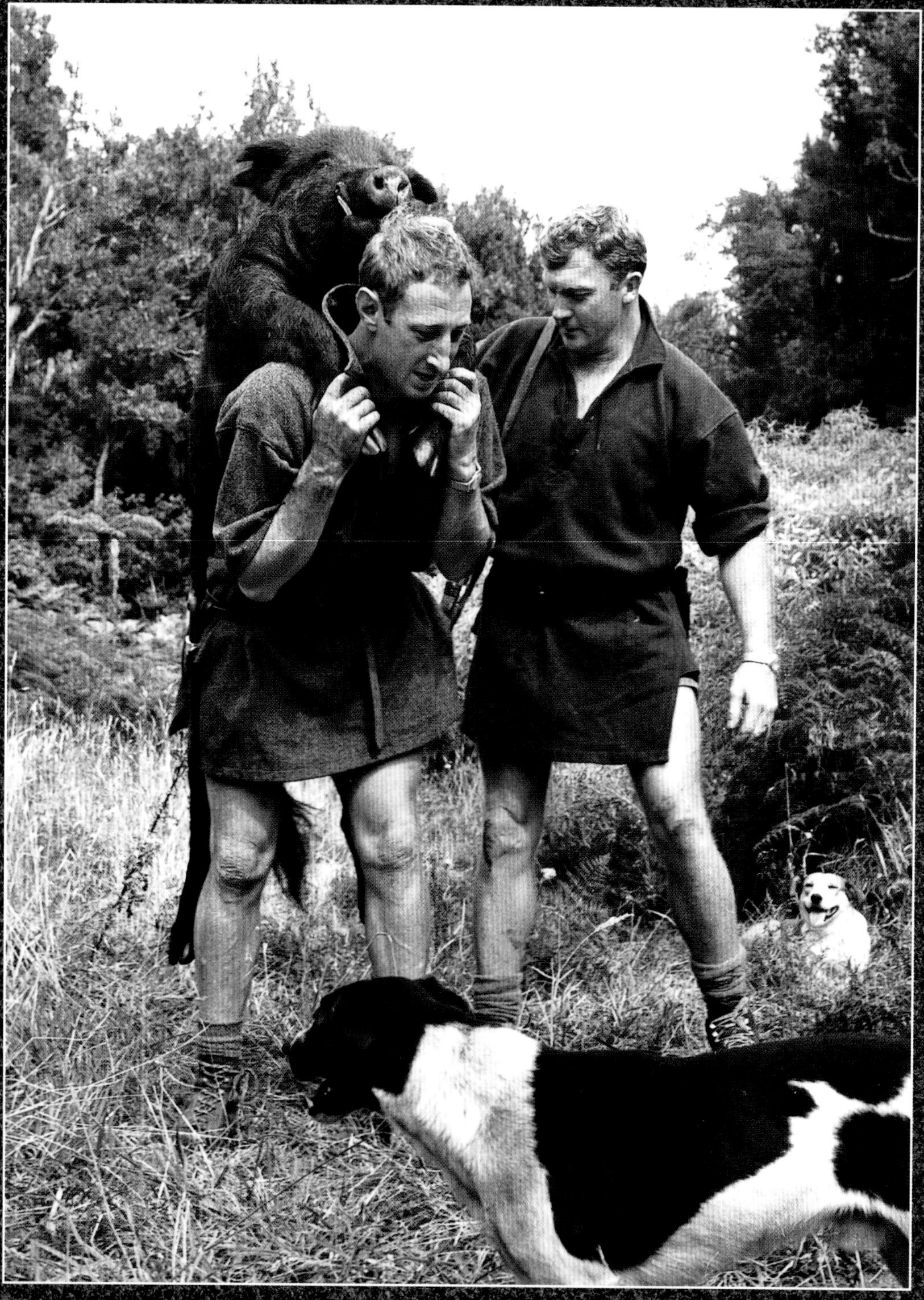

Chapter 2
A Good Keen Man

For the next few years my life was filled with mountains and bush and rivers, rain and snow and ice and sweat. I shot deer in most back-country areas of New Zealand. There were deer everywhere. Most of the men who hunted had been caught up in the war and the only times much of the country was hunted at all was by old-timers, trophy-hunters who usually carried an old Long-Tom rifle with a five-shot magazine. They'd shoot a young hind and hang it up for meat and then wouldn't fire another unless they stalked a stag with a bigger head than the ones they had on the wall of the shed at home.

– The Life and Times of a Good Keen Man

SELWYN BUCKNELL
(Former Field Officer)

In the early fifties there were not really a lot of us full-time government hunters on deer control and we were spread out over the land, but there was an incredible grapevine which spread word of the tallies and activities of other hunters. I knew people who worked with Barry Crump. He started very young on deer control and he used old Ted Rye as his mentor.

Crumpy's first book was a roll-on from Ted Rye's stories – that's most certainly where Barry got a lot of them from. For example, that one with the pigs hanging over the bloody cliff and all that type of carry-on, that was Ted Rye's story and Crumpy used it. That was okay. But as Crumpy got older and more into his game, the stories were his; they became more and more his own.

Later on I got Crumpy together in the pub with two of his old bosses from the deerculling days. There was my great friend Morris John (Red) Fairhall, who was Crumpy's first field officer when he went to the bush, and Ted Rye, who was the senior field officer. We had a hell of a good time.

It turned out Crump was so grubby and untidy and untrained around camp that Ted wanted to sack him. A lot of us old proper deercullers, we were tidy, we looked after ourselves. You had some fellas, their camps were that dirty they got boils. They didn't look after themselves, everything was scruffy, there were bits of meat hanging outside the camp with maggots on them, things like that. Morris John Fairhall wouldn't put up with that, but

I spent quite a lot of time on my own that first season, or maybe I noticed it more. The first few weeks were the worst. I didn't know what I was doing and had to make it up as I went along. I rigged up a disgraceful tent-camp on a beech bushline at a place called The Hoggett and made disgraceful loaves of camp-oven bread over disgraceful fires. I groan aloud as I think of the camp, it was even in a disgraceful place.

When I returned to The Hoggett I found that the Field Officer had been and left a load of supplies and a note going crook about the disgraceful state of the camp and saying that he was bringing my mate in next time he came. The note didn't say when that would be. In fact it was some weeks before he brought in my experienced mate and told me to see how he worked out and left us to it.

– The Life and Times of a Good Keen Man

Ted Rye was the boss, and he loved Crumpy and wouldn't let Red sack him. Crump must have learned to tidy his camp up a bit, but he was still a young man then.

I think he was the second youngest deerculler ever. It wasn't everybody who could hack it in the bush. You'd go in for a trip and emerge into town five months later, and sometimes you'd been on your own all that time.

We got supplied with pack horses then, but on a lot of the blocks you couldn't get pack horses in – it was all tracked up the back of Waikaremoana, in the Ureweras. But it wasn't that rugged for a young guy like Crumpy. It was wonderful for him, he was doing what he wanted to do.

I didn't actually come face to face with Barry until one morning in 1966 when I was the district wildlife ranger at Waikaremoana. I was preparing my work boat when I heard a voice behind me.

"Gidday," Crump said, like all us back country fellas, "any chance of a lift up the lake with you?"

I turned around and shook hands with him and said okay, but I'd be away all day.

I liked the man, we got on fine. He wasn't working, he just wanted to get out for a bit. By then I think he'd published about three books. He was a real ragamuffin, but man to man he was a good fellow. I was checking licences and weighing fish and so on, talking to people, and he was just there, he never poked his nose in at all. Next time I went up he came out with me again and we stayed overnight way out at the back of the lake.

He was great company, with none of the big 'I am' side of him coming out. It did a bit later, though, when I had to weigh in the trout for one of the angling club competitions. It was rather a snobby outfit with a palatial hut on the lake shore.

In walked Barry with this gorgeous redheaded lady. He was a real show-off.

"You all know me," he growled. Then he turned to the lady. "She's the best root this side of the black stump," he announced.

Well, you can imagine the shocked looks on the faces of some of these upper-class ladies. Most of them there came round, though, and had a great evening with Crump. If he had a crew around you could see him sort of expand and gather people in.

I met Barry again when he came to live in Havelock just a couple of years ago. By that time I'd retired. I banged into him in the pub. "Gidday," he said, and we sat down and had a few drinks. A couple of days later he said, "Hey, Buck, none of these bastards around here know me, and this new gun licence, I've got to get somebody to give me a letter." I found this rather ridiculous, that I gave the famous hunter Barry Crump a letter so he could get a gun licence.

Barry and I spent a lot of time together when he lived in Havelock, for maybe a year and a half. We were near enough neighbours, but we met in the pub; we didn't go to each other's homes a lot. What he did was he'd get himself half-shickered in the afternoon down at the pub, go home and have a big sleep, and wake up and start writing.

As a person Crumpy was what he appeared to be – he really was a good keen man. Soldiers have something, seamen have something when they're together; well, it's the same with us fellas. What we share is a feeling I don't think anyone could describe unless they've been in the bush too. What it feels like not to come out for five months and most of that time you're on your own. A couple of times in the pub old Crumpy put his arm around me and said, "Buck, they don't know, do they?"

And they just don't.

JACK LASENBY
(Hunter and Writer)

We were just kids really when I met Barry Crump. We were both deerculling: I was at Waikaremoana and Barry was over at the Waiau River. He'd been shooting for a year or so when I first went there, but I'd never know what Barry was really up to, he was a bullshit artist. I mean it in a nice way. The first time I talked to him he bullshitted me that he'd just come back from the Korean War where a lot of the other jokers had been.

I was in the Urewera for about ten years altogether, culling and possuming. Barry was on and off again possuming and of course knocked around the bush occasionally for the rest of his life. There's a vast difference between the sentimentalised Crumpy you see on television with Lloyd Scott and the Crump that I remember and that most of the chaps would have known in the bush. He was a much more complex person, a real human being rather than the mythologised figure, although it's been self-mythologising to a large extent of course.

Something that I've often thought about was that, of the crowd of us in the Urewera at that time, at least half a dozen of us – Rex Forrester, Mike Bennet, Don Kiddy, Alan Farmer, Crump and myself – have published books and papers, almost all of them to do with the bush. It's interesting that out of a relatively small number of people there should be so many published.

The connection was probably Ted Rye, our senior field officer, who was the greatest yarn spinner of all time, I think, brilliant.

There's a marvellous bullshit touch just tossed off in a line or two in Barry's first book about how he shot a big stag on dusk and couldn't get down off the tops in the dark. The temperature had dropped below freezing point, so he gutted the stag, crawled in and slept inside it. That was a wonderful bullshit story of Ted's that went on for an hour or a couple of hours, depending on how pissed or how talkative he was. Barry used it, as he did several of Ted's stories, and I don't mean that as a criticism at all. I was astonished by the brilliance with which Barry took a yarn like that and did it so obliquely and cleverly in a few sentences.

It was a superb story and I've wondered about it for years. Then when I was editing the *School Journal* I went mad on Eskimo stories and folk stories in general. I came across a marvellous Eskimo version of the story about a polar bear instead of a stag and I wondered how in hell that tale came down to Ted. He certainly shoved the story onto us, relating it to our circumstances, setting his version up in the head of Clarence in the Inland Kaikouras, and told it absolutely convincingly.

Barry once asked me years later what it was we had in common, all us young jokers. We were all looking for our old man, for a father, said Barry. We thought back to the lot of us – it wasn't everybody of course, like any generalisation – but it was an accurate observation after I'd thought about it for a while. And then Barry said, "Of course, we all fastened onto old Ted as our father, the poor bastard."

There was some truth in that. Old Ted wasn't all roses and laughter by any means, but I think he was one of the three most intelligent people I've known in my life, an extraordinary man. I've never seen anybody with such powers of observation as he had.

I don't know how many of those jokers would agree with me about Ted Rye or would have thought about it afterwards. As a writer and as a teacher I've had to, because kids and teachers are forever saying to writers, "Where did you begin to write?" I know the importance of modelling in education or in behaviour generally, and I suspect that the extraordinary model of our senior field officer was a huge influence on Barry, as he was on all of us. We loathed him at times, he was the most difficult man. I think he was bedevilled by mood swings. At one end of the range he told those stories. At the other end he lapsed into silence, was dreadful, intolerable company and used that silence as a power over us. We called Ted the Grey Ghost and we made up stories about the Grey Ghost.

Barry had natural story-telling ability anyway, but I think Ted probably nurtured and encouraged that in him. I think he had an enormous effect on Barry. His old man was alive but Barry didn't seem to think much of him in those early years. He spoke warmly of his mother towards the end of his life, but I remember him turning up at Ruatahuna with a bag full of religious tracts his mother had given him and telling me how he'd stuffed a pile of them in the culvert coming into Ruatahuna because he didn't want the boys to know.

I met his sister Carol when I was in hospital once with a cut hand, and she was a lovely, open young girl, very pleasant indeed, and told me how she and Barry used to play tig. She would have been just a kid, of course, and he'd be getting on the bus at Otahuhu with his old rifle and pack and they'd be tigging each other last. He'd tig her, tear along the road and jump on the bus as it was pulling away, and she'd see him grinning at her out the back window. She didn't seem to have any idea of the sort of life he lived, probably none of the family did at that time. It was a very lonely, dangerous life and yet she saw her brother as like another big child acting the goat.

Barry and I used to talk about writing. I remember one of the first indications of his future as a writer (with hindsight, of course) was when we were across the lake one winter together and putting in a track across to Waireka Station. I had several books in my gear, including Joyce's *Ulysses* and Pound's *Seventy Cantos* and I remember Crump reading them and commenting on them intelligently, which was certainly unusual in the bush. Even having the interest to begin with was unusual, but he had no trouble at all reading them.

Later we went possuming together, working up the Horomanga in the Urewera. He got married to Tina Anso and left the bush and only came back occasionally possuming, and I saw less and less of him. But we retained a friendship.

In the early sixties I spent some time in Auckland and had a room in Grafton Road in that area now taken over by the university. Barry arrived

They were tough old rags, those mountain men. Tea and rice and salt were their main supplies. Imagine what they thought of us louts. Condensed milk, tinned cheese, army biscuits, ten-shot magazines, shooting everything that moved, hinds and all! We were ruining the back-country. Beneath contempt. Pansies!

– *The Life and Times of a Good Keen Man*

with the manuscript of *A Good Keen Man*. Reading through the draft, I didn't have enough nous myself to see what an enormous seller it was going to be. I knew a fair bit about literature but I had no commercial acumen. As well I stood too close to the experience he'd described in the book. I was reading it to see myself, or seeing myself in every second character and recognising all the pieces that he put together into the composites that most characters are in fiction, identifying the boys, the watersheds, the rivers, the lake. I really wasn't a very good judge of it at all. In no time the book had come out and was an instant best seller.

The Forestry Department took over culling in '56 from Internal Affairs, and among the boys that stayed on culling and the forestry chaps that went on to it, there was a great deal of envy of Crump over that book and quite an amount of ill-feeling. Recently I was listening to one of the Spectrum radio documentaries, *Tales from the Back Country*, and one of the old Forestry blokes was talking about being up the Whirinaki at Minginui when the book came out and how much resentment there was among the boys. A lot of them haven't forgiven Crump, they said he was skiting and showing off and claiming he'd shot more deer than he had, which was perfectly true but has nothing whatsoever to do with a work of fiction.

It's still a considerable piece of writing and that attitude, that selfishness, wasn't the tall poppy syndrome. The problem was that Crump had broken outside an understanding, broken a barrier, by talking about their world. And those jokers, of course, were totally unused to the nature of fiction.

The first book was a greater success than anyone could have foreseen and Barry's life changed overnight. He came under the immense pressure of public notoriety and he said to me on a number of occasions that he didn't cope very well with it. I don't know who would be likely to cope – having a hell of a lot of women flinging themselves at him, having his pockets full of money and a reputation which he himself helped foster.

I didn't tell Ted Rye that Barry had used some of the stories that he used to tell but I knew that he would find out sooner or later. No doubt he did but he never commented on it, it just wouldn't have been his way.

We remained friends. Crump was essentially the same person but he took on that created persona if necessary in public. A few years later when I was married and was living in Devonport, Crump came back from Aussie. He'd just published *Gulf* and he stayed in the bach at the end of our section and wrote *Scrapwagon*. I remember going down to the pub with him one night and somebody came up to him.

"How would you like that?" Barry said to me afterwards. "You can't go anywhere without somebody who has to come up to speak to you." Nine times out of ten it was just somebody who wanted to shake hands, he said, and tell you about their uncle who was a hell of a character, but every tenth one was some joker who wanted to out-shoot the fastest gun in the West. You got good at picking them out and belting them before they could belt you, he said, but you still missed out every now and again and got some fearful thrashings.

Sam Hunt said much the same thing when he and Gary McCormick began their readings in pubs. Sam is very similar in many ways to Barry in aspects of his personality and his ability to turn his life experience into literature and literature into entertainment, which I admire immensely in both Barry and Sam. But they've done it outside the normal conventions, at considerable expense of spirit, and both have been shunned to some extent by the academic world as a result. I think that is a great pity because it's led to a failure of recognition of what is of quality in their work.

And yet I can't think of anybody before Barry who was recognised so widely through New Zealand because of his writing. Barry suffered that sort of popularity and I think it threw strains upon his relationships with almost everybody. Like most writers, I think, Barry got a gutsful of people who wanted to know him rather than to read his books. It was easy enough for his mates from the bush to cut him down or pull him back into line when he got a bit too carried away with his own importance and yet he kept up those friendships and, as far as I remember, they were very important to him. We remain a close-knit group after all these years.

I think the last time I saw Crump was down at Opotiki. I'd been fishing in the Urewera and walked down from the bush and called on him there. We were in touch through other mates and I'd get the odd message and the occasional letter. He wrote when I published *The Lake*, my first novel.

I read most of his books. I had my favourites, probably the first two, *A Good Keen Man* and *Hang on a Minute Mate*; and there were a couple of brilliant short stories in *Warm Beer*. The one that starts 'Young Davey Hill was as keen on dogs as a starving tapeworm', about the chap who cut the throats on everything that moves, is a very black story. It surprises me it's not better known.

And his picture of Big Nud living in that coal and farming valley during the Depression, the way he terrorised all the local people, that's a beautifully written story. The sound of the iron wheels of the heavy dray he drove around the district was enough in itself to scare people. Visiting women when their men were down the mines who were too scared to say anything when their husbands came home. It is a sort of personality Crump understood very well himself. There was something of the sinister in him at times. I suppose it's the old thing, you've got to find the criminal inside yourself to understand the criminal and write about it.

And I enjoyed *Wild Pork and Watercress*. Like a lot of Crump's writing, it gives that wonderful appearance of having been tossed off, but of course it was the result of a hell of a lot of hard work. I can remember Barry sitting up on the bed in the bach at Devonport writing into a hard-backed exercise book. Ballpoints were still comparatively new to us and we were finding them unsatisfactory – our writing became so untidy until we learned to control them – and we were trying out all the new fibre tip and felt tip pens. We were swapping them as we got new ones and trying them out.

He worked very hard at *Scrapwagon*, trying bits out, coming down to the house and discussing passages with me, reading them aloud, and often I was aware when he was telling me a story he'd be sounding out how it went. There's a simple sentence in one of his books, 'Crossing the river was as cold as an axe head.' That is such a brilliant, sharp, poetic image it might have just occurred to him, but it's much more likely to be the product of rewriting and rewriting and rewriting. That's the usual way you come into that very sharp imagery.

He would say something like, "It's just something I wrote in a couple of weeks." It might be true of some of them, because he did become extremely repetitive, working over virtually the same material. But he'd know as well as anyone else that a great deal of your writing has been worked over in your head both consciously and unconsciously long before you put anything on paper. And he'd say something like that as a way of adding to the romantic bushman image.

KEVIN IRELAND
(Writer)

It's absurd to think that you can describe a person's life in a single word, but knowing that has never stopped anyone from trying, so if there is one word I was forced to choose to sum up every aspect of Barry's life and character it would be: *unforgettable* – and I'm not the only one to think so.

The instant I met him forty years ago – and, remember, he would have been a mere twenty-one or twenty-two, and I was only a year or two older – I was bowled over by Barry. It was a meeting that would impact in several ways on both of us, but for me it is still this feeling of unforgettability that lingers down the years as my most powerful impression of him.

Now let me put that remark in an entirely different context. In Barry's most confusing work of history and mystery – his autobiography *The Life and Times of a Good Keen Man* – he writes how he and his wife of the time turned up in London in the early 1970s and stayed with me, and how much he liked the London scene, with all "the lanes and pubs and colourful people". Then he says he took off for Germany, decided to go to India alone, by motorbike, and he packed up his wife and kids and sent them back to me. So far, so true. But what he shyly leaves out, though it's an element that puts an entirely different complexion on the story, is that the best part of a year later he paid me a second visit.

I had rung Barry in Auckland to tell him that his wife and kids were in a small spot of bother, and there was no way out of it, he had to drop

Among my new friends were a bunch of young blokes who were starting up a literary magazine called *Mate*. It was one of them, Kevin, who talked me into having a go at writing a short story, and they published it. I was a bit surprised at how easy the writing of it was. Kevin had a large collection of books and I soaked them up almost as he recommended them. Caxton, Dickens, Lamb, Trollope, Lear, Mark Twain, Lewis Carroll, Banjo Paterson, Butler, Leacock, Saki, Thurber, Dylan Thomas, Waugh, Kingsley Amis, Joyce Carey, Aldous Huxley, Nancy Mitford, Wodehouse and many others.

– *The Life and Times of a Good Keen Man*

everything, jump on the next plane and come and pick them up. He didn't argue the point. He got on a plane and shot straight over. When I got back home from work on the day he arrived, I found a note to let me know he'd beaten me there by a few minutes, he was dying of thirst and if I cared to follow him he'd be down at my local pub. I went there, and found him chatting to the barmaid – of course.

"You won't believe this, Kev," he said as soon as he saw me. "Do you know what's happened? I walked in the door and I found this lady here had just poured me a pint of Guinness. She said she saw me coming down the street, and she remembered that was my favourite drink."

"Just doing my job," the barmaid said.

"Doing your job?" Barry asked. "You're working in the busiest pub in this part of London, you've got the choice of a dozen brands of beer on draught, you haven't seen me in nearly a year, yet you remembered my drink was a pint of Guinness."

"I'd only need to meet you once," she said, "and I'd always remember you. You're unforgettable."

She wasn't just being polite, she had recalled him immediately all that time later from thousands of passing customers. Even in a London throng he was unforgettable. Of all Barry's many attributes, the one thing everyone would have to agree on was that he stuck forever in the memory.

But the implications don't end there. That story tells us a lot about the strange *reliability* that was a basic part of Barry's character – a character, I might say, that was far more complex than most people thought. Barry often, and understandably, comes in for a bit of stick over the way he set up home with a number of women, was a father figure to the best part of a cricket team of sons, then always shot through. It was weird to watch, but let's face all the facts. It's easy to forget that it was just as weird that there was a queue of women out there who were always willing, *knowingly*, to take on the hopeless job of attempting to supply a cure. They joined him like accomplices.

In many people's book Barry was a man who got fonged, missed appointments and could beat the great Houdini at the disappearing act – to such people he was unreliability personified. Okay, the faults are undeniable, but what I'm getting at is that this aspect of his character has to be balanced against another side: in my experience, he was possessed of an indomitable, though highly contradictory, dependability. When I phoned him and explained the situation his wife and kids were in, Crump came to the rescue without hesitation, without a single moan. That didn't mean he was going to set up home with them again, but it did mean he'd be right at hand to get them out of a real fix. And, to cap off the story, he could only afford a single to get to London, so I had to lend him nearly all the spending money I'd saved for a trip back to Auckland which my wife and kids and I were going to make a few months later.

The outcome was that not long after I arrived back home, I was summoned out to Henderson for a cup of tea and a yarn. The day passed and neither of us brought up the subject of the money. As I was leaving, he shoved a roll in my pocket. Nothing was said. That was his style.

You didn't easily discover that side to Barry. He spent a great deal of his life obscuring his tracks, and the soft, generous, dependable side often got hidden. He had been brought up in a Puritan tradition, and it was almost as if the transparent goodness in him was a source of irritation – as sometimes were the details of his life that put him in a better light than he felt he deserved.

One of the features of Barry's life as a writer was his modesty. That may seem a strange remark to those who remember him as a great deal larger than life – which indeed he was – but it needs to be stressed. Barry never boasted about his immense abilities. He was proud of his twenty-four book titles and million-plus buyers, he was proud that he was the one living New Zealand writer to make it onto a postage stamp, proud of the gong the Governor-General gave him, proud that the Toyota advertisements revived his reputation as a television star, but he never went around banging a drum about his achievements.

Barry was always a bit bemused by his success; he was happy with it, but he never took it for granted, and that meant he never got big-headed about it. Three or four years ago I had my last long sober chat with him – there was a later meeting over drinks, but that was a bit blurry for both of us. Among the topics of conversation, we talked about his books and he said he was pretty pleased about the way things had gone, but that he often thought he might have done a bit more work on this book or that, to make it better than it was. Yet he kept on saying that there was always the next one. That was the one he was interested in. Perhaps it would be the book he'd be really pleased with.

The one thing that really did get under his skin was the snobbery that he'd been shown on several occasions by twerps who should have known better. One well-known writer once referred to him as an anecdotal ape, and the remark hurt. It was unjust, unkind and – more than that – it was utterly untrue.

Barry was one of our finest-ever writers and he will remain so. He wasn't just a collector of anecdotes or an isolated literary freak. He placed himself in the mainstream of the longest tradition in world literature, among the fablers and raconteurs. In ancient times he would have been the man who sat by the fire and told spellbinding tales of deeds and misdeeds that celebrated the comic triumphs and the endurances which gave identity to the tribe – what the Irish call a *sonnachie*. Modern examples of this tradition would have to include writers of world stature such as Mark Twain and Henry Lawson, and in New Zealand such popular interpreters of the vernacular as Frank Anthony, who in the 1920s wrote the marvellous *Me and Gus* stories, and Ronald Hugh Morrieson, who wrote *Scarecrow* and *Came a Hot Friday*.

Barry was a leader in a tradition that has a genius for giving an oblique angle to the everyday incident that touches our lives, our souls and our concepts of ourselves. But to achieve this leadership he required more than just a wonderful ear for the rhythms of everyday speech and a natural instinct for the way to pitch a story – he had to be also an extremely gifted stylist. The way he constructed his narratives made them ring true.

To put it another way: he's had lots of imitators, but there's still only one authentic Crump. To write like that, first of all you need the skeleton of experience, then you have to apply the flesh of words to that experience, then you need the ability to shape your material into a body of work. It all comes down to translating events into language, and the truth of the matter is that, though most people think they've got at least one book inside them, they haven't – they may have had adventures interesting enough to fill a book, but they lack the gift to shape the words.

Barry had that gift – and I had the pure luck to have the sense to see it shining out of him when we first met.

In the acknowledgement at the beginning of A Good Keen Man, Barry wrote: "My thanks are due to the Wildlife Branch of Internal Affairs, for its unwitting assistance in providing materials for this book, to Kevin Ireland, who insisted that I start work thereon, and to Alex Fry, who gave invaluable help towards its completion." And there's a story behind those statements too.

I did fire up Barry to write down his adventures and yarns, and Alex Fry did help knock Barry's manuscript into final shape at Reeds publishing house. But there was more to it than that, and it happened this way.

We met at a party in Grafton Road, when it was the bed-sitter capital of Auckland, and after listening to a few of his yarns, I collared him and told him he was going to start writing – or, if he didn't, then I would, if he was willing to talk to me at dictation speed. I promised him he'd make a fortune.

In his biography, Barry records that he met his first wife at a party "where one of the shooters introduced me to a woman who I thought was pretty beaut". That is a slip of the pen. He met her also at the same party. I had gone there with a group of friends that included Tina Anso – who, by the way, didn't know any shooters at the time – and I introduced them. A couple of months later they were married. It turned out, in hindsight, to be one of Barry's big nights, so he can be forgiven for a bit of interior decorating.

Tina's mother Ruby owned a typewriter, so Barry borrowed it, set it up in the living room and we wrote the first drafts of Barry's first story together – a bit like riding a tandem bicycle, except that he did all the pedalling, while I did the steering.

I had kept on drumming into him that he was going to be a writer and I'd also got him to think long-term about a major work, so he was all primed and ready to go. He told me he was confident he could write a book about deerculling, and he'd string his adventures around the way one of his field officers was always sending him good keen men to work with. He would call the book *A Good Keen Man*. So we agreed we'd get started and I said I'd type, while he recited, just to give him the hang of things.

It was hilarious. As soon as Barry knew I was ready to type, he changed his voice and his vocabulary. The only people he'd talked to before in an arrangement like this had been policemen. I had to insist that I'd only tap out words as he really spoke them. So every time he'd come to a point in the story and wander off into words that went something like: "On the afternoon of the aforementioned day when the aforesaid Legs and myself were proceeding towards the dwelling . . .", I'd have to stop him and yell, "Cut it out, Crumpy. We're trying to write a book, not a bloody police report."

After two or three days of this, and starting stories that didn't get finished till much later, we finished the first version of the story that eventually became the "I Meet Legs" chapter in *A Good Keen Man*.

We had several goes at the story over the next few days, and after we'd more or less given it a shaping up, Barry said he was confident he'd got the idea of how to put the words down himself, and he thought he ought to take over the controls on his own. So I dropped out altogether, and it wasn't till some weeks later that I asked how he was getting on with the big project, and he said he'd slowed up. It was harder than he'd thought.

The only way I could help him with the problem he'd run into was to

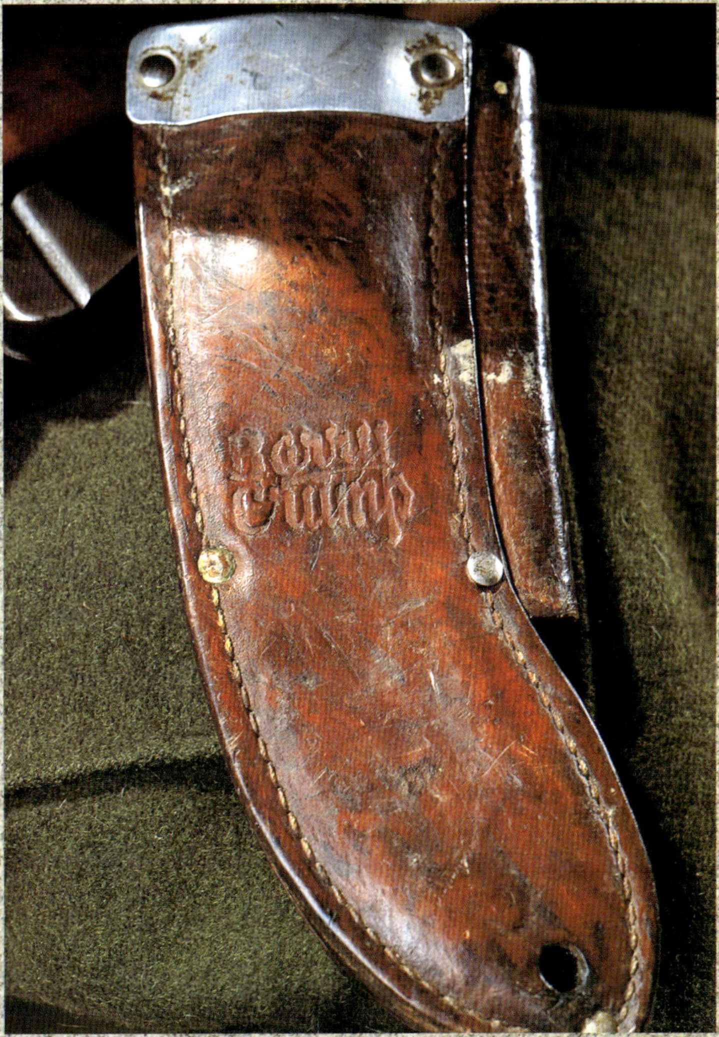

tell him that just about every good writer in the world also happened to be a good reader. He may have managed to pick up a few elementary wrinkles from me, but he was going to learn his craft properly only by total immersion in books. He'd get it right by seeing how others had done it before him, then by working out his own path.

In those days I spent my money only on beer and books, so I had a big and broad library, and Barry asked if I'd be willing to let him come and do a bit of borrowing. Of course, I said yes.

A little while later he turned up outside my place with a small, battered truck – no Hilux in those days – piled up with empty apple cases.

"I've come for the books," he said. "I've got this hut in the Waitakeres, so I thought I'd take your advice and I'd just sit out there and read day and night."

I waved at my bookshelves and told him to make a selection.

"A selection?" he said. "I've come for the lot. That's what the truck and the apple cases are for."

Months later he came back with every book packed up neatly again. I asked if he'd really managed to get through them.

"Yes, all of them," he said.

"The Sterne, Joyce, Byron, Hazlitt, Swift . . . ?" I asked.

"Every one of them. Cover to cover," he replied.

I was staggered. I'd lent him books I hadn't got around to reading myself, yet he'd holed up like a hermit in the hills, and he hadn't left off till he'd devoured every page.

Now that story tells us two things that have never been acknowledged about Barry. One myth (which he helped create) is that he found writing easy, but the truth is that for years he worked like a slave at becoming a writer. And another myth is that he wrote like an innocent, without knowing a thing about his craft, but in fact he cultivated literary friends such as myself, Maurice Duggan, James K. Baxter and a host of others, and he studied the way other writers had gone about their work. He tapped deep into the whole tradition of world literature, consumed with curiosity and hunger, as well as plain ambition. Let's get this right once and for all, Barry was a dedicated literary man, he did his homework. He wasn't a writer by some sort of fluke – he was a worker, he was devoted to his craft. I saw the whole thing happen.

Yet you'll find that Barry was always taken seriously when he made off-the-cuff remarks, such as how he'd decided to write because he'd read a book about deerculling and he thought he could turn out a better one. Or you'll read, repeated again and again, how it took him about a month to write *A Good Keen Man*. To which the only answer is: when you consider his character, you'd expect him to say those things, wouldn't you?

The truth is that he began *A Good Keen Man* the day he and I got Tina's mother's typewriter going in that New Lynn sitting room in 1957, and he worked, on and off, at his manuscript, with long periods of intense effort, finishing it towards the middle or end of 1959.

Some of the later books may indeed have been written in one short burst of great activity, but by then Barry had the knack and he set his sights sometimes on doing no more than what was needed. His early work was ambitious – he was *determined* to succeed – and he accomplished his ambition by labour and concentration.

And here's another point. Ray Richards, who worked at Reeds when the book was accepted, was quoted in the Herald obituary as saying that one of the things Alex Fry (Who gave an editorial polish to Barry's completed manuscript) had managed to accomplish was to change the narrative from the third person to the first. That may well be true, though I'd like to see the manuscript evidence to prove it. When Barry published the "I Meet Legs" chapter as a short story (under the title A Good Keen Man!) it was definitely not in the third person, but in the first – just as he had always planned the book to be. Perhaps he did change the whole book later to the third person, but that would have involved a huge amount of rewriting and it certainly went right against the whole shape and logic of the story as he outlined it in the beginning. The narrative simply has to be in the first person.

This may seem to be a small point, but it's essential to delve into these things and ask for the evidence. A little thing like that is quite likely to alter your observations.

It's also essential always to keep in mind a couple of other very important basic facts. The first is that there was nothing fake or put on about Barry. There was certainly a public-performance side to his character, and he loved to play to the gallery, but he wasn't a gifted actor like Scotty. Underneath the act, Barry was for real. He simply did a footlights version of *himself*. He wouldn't have been any good either as Hamlet or his father's ghost.

Nothing he wrote about was untrue to the nature of his experience or to his imagination. He was a superb bushman. Again, I have first-hand proof of this. I spent occasions possum trapping with him for weeks in the Ureweras, which is among the hardest stretches of country to work in the North Island. We lived off the flour, sugar and tea we carried in, and the deer we shot. His bushcraft was brilliant. And he was a wonderful, dependable mate to share a camp with.

The first time we went in, he picked a great campsite on high ground by a river. He got me to get our tarpaulin out and cut manuka poles, and while I did so, he felled a kahikatea so that it dropped, with an accuracy you could measure to the inch, right on to a large boulder, where it shattered all along its length as though it had been cut into planks. Barry chopped these into slabs to build the walls of the camp and a chimney, then up went the ridgepole for the tarpaulin. We built bunks, cut pigfern for our mattresses and we had our first meal of camp-oven bread and venison back steaks just on sundown – all after a long and difficult tramp in.

I've never seen anything like it. Expert work with the axe, a plan in his head of what he was doing, damn-all talk and not a single physical movement wasted. His mastery of the complicated Urewera gully and ridge structure was absolutely uncanny. He *belonged* in the bush. He was part of it. At any given moment he could stop with animal instinct and know where he was, and he gave you the confidence – and the bushcraft – to be able to go out on possum lines on your own and never get lost.

The only thing I did to repay him for the experience, which no tramping club in the country could ever have supplied me with, was to teach him to play chess. We were stretched out by the fire, drinking tea and yarning one night, when I remarked it was a wonder to me that he and his mates had never thought of playing chess.

Barry's reaction was instant. "Teach me," he demanded.

I pointed out that we had no board and it would take a week to carve a rough set of chessmen.

"It'll take an hour," he said. "I'll carve lines on a lump of timber for a chess board. We've got a pen, so we can ink in the black squares."

"That's the easy bit. What about the chessmen?" I asked.

"Use these," he said and, with a marvellous bit of lateral thinking, he tossed me a couple of candles. "Start melting them and mould a set of chessmen with your fingers. We'll spill ink on one lot, too, so we can tell the difference."

It was a number-eight fencing-wire solution, but a brilliant one, and he stayed enthusiastic about the game – even though a few days later he told me, just as we were setting off to check our lines in the morning, "You know, Kev, I feel knackered before I start." I asked him what the matter was, and he said, "It's the third time in a row I haven't had a proper sleep. I've been dreaming bloody chess moves, non-stop, all night."

There were suggestions in the past that Barry must have had ghost writers and that he exaggerated his stories of the bush. Both these rumours have faded, but they've never quite gone away. So it's a good time to insist again that he learned to write the hard way. He was never too proud to be helped or to take advice when getting started, but the words were all his, every one of them. And, as for the stories, he worked by illumination, not by exaggeration – except for the occasional comic effect. If anything, Barry's stories were often underplayed or reshaped to minimise the dangers they described and to highlight their entertainment value, so that no one would think he was running away with his fantasies.

Yet there *were* extraordinarily fantastic and sometimes dark sides to some of his writing. One of the best short stories of the past forty years is

Young Davey Hill was as keen on dogs as a starving tapeworm. He often had two or three hidden in the scrub along the big swamp and up the gully behind his father's homestead. Mongrels of all sizes and description that were surreptitiously fed from Davey's plate and late-night milkings of the house cow when he couldn't get scraps for them anywhere else. On an average of about once a month his father would hear Davey's dogs barking at night or catch him sneaking out to feed them, and another batch of stray mongrels would be released with a boot in the ribs and shouted and stoned off the place – on to somebody else's. Even Davey couldn't say where all these dogs came from. They just turned up and, in time, were turned out again.

– Bedtime Yarns

one that turned up in the Otago University magazine in 1963. It is called "...That Way" and it begins with the wonderful line: "Young Davey Hill was as keen on dogs as a starving tapeworm", and it goes on to describe how two rabbiters have a bit of murderous trouble with their dogs, their dog-tucker and then each other, before it ends with the equally brilliant line: " 'Never thought you'd go that way, boy,' he said in the voice he reserved for special occasions." It's grim, gothic, scary, and worthy of Henry Lawson at his best – yet it's also distorted in a brilliantly surreal way that comes within an ace of mad comedy. Or there's the part in *Hang on a Minute Mate* where Sam is in gaol, reflecting on his mateship with Jack, and he says: "I really got saddled with him in the finish. Couldn't move but what Jack was hanging around watching everything a man did. Like a young dog or something. And we weren't getting anywhere – neither of us." These are just brief glimpses of the moodier, deeper aspect of Barry's genius that have so far had little attention.

And this leads on to another comment that seems to me to be important when we talk about the real Barry we knew, and that's the way he came among us almost as though he had stepped magically out of our past, out of an ancestral legend. I took him to meet Frank Sargeson and afterwards, when I asked Frank what he made of him, he exclaimed that the man was extraordinary. "He's an anachronism," he said. "He speaks like an echo of our past."

That was part of the Crump secret – the way he represented in his writings and in his physical presence a romantic notion we have of ourselves as having descended from larger and better people than we are, people who had simpler and more solid verities, people who were rough, dependable, maybe a bit cranky, but always self-reliant and never whinging. Yet it was more than that. In all his best writing, however rumbustious or funny, there is always a heavy air of nostalgia – a hankering after, and a sadness for, what's forever past and lost.

It's the way I feel about Barry now. I think there's a lot to regret in the way he became isolated from most other writers and felt a bit sidelined and put down by some. He did more than enough in his lifetime to have deserved an honorary doctorate from one of our universities. That would have gone some way to making up for the neglect. He touched an area of our private notions of ourselves in a luminous, ludicrous, comic way that no other New Zealand writer has done. His words celebrate our slap-dash, contrary, proud uniqueness as a people. He got a lot of the characters we can still meet in bush huts and city streets absolutely spot on.

Barry invented nothing – especially in himself. He lived and wrote as he was, and never changed. And when we saw him flying through the air in his Hilux, it was as if he knew that we knew he never needed wings. Crumpy was the genuine article.

RAY RICHARDS
(ORIGINAL PUBLISHER OF BARRY CRUMP'S BOOKS)

BARRY CRUMP TWICE OFFERED *A GOOD KEEN MAN* TO PUBLISHER PAUL'S BOOK ARCADE AND THEY REJECTED IT TWICE. THE THIRD REJECTION WAS FROM WHITCOMBE AND TOMBS, AUCKLAND, WHO REPLIED BY LETTER, 13 JULY 1959.

"We thank you for submitting your MS which we have read with interest. We regret, however, we are unable to undertake the publication as the cost would not make it a profitable proposition for either you or ourselves."

When Crump offered his single-spaced, shop-soiled *A Good Keen Man* to AH & AW Reed, Wellington, I was the publisher, and I had no hesitation in accepting the ugly duckling manuscript for publication. To turn it into a publishing swan I changed the narrator from Jack Somebody to Barry Crump himself, so that the book became the fictional autobiography of the author, who had no problem assuming the new person, indeed he revelled in it. Crump was the Good Keen Man for the rest of his life. What a lucky break.

To effect the switch from a third-person narrative to the first person, and to polish and shape the manuscript, I asked *Listener* staffer Alex Fry to edit, which he did superbly.

The finishing touch was the unusual decision to illustrate the novel with line drawings by Dennis Turner, who gave visual form, location and drama to the fact, fun and fables of A Good Keen Man and his mates. The illustrations added visual appeal and credibility and bulked the short novel out to full fiction length.

The rest is history.

Thirty-seven years later, 300,000 copies later and six million dollars (retail value) later, the Whitcombe rejection of *A Good Keen Man* ranks among the worst publishing decisions of all time. A couple of dozen further Crump books followed *A Good Keen Man*.

The same Reed formula applied to the second Crump manuscript, *Hang on a Minute Mate*, with Alex Fry polishing the text and Dennis Turner giving visual shape to Crump's great characters.

Thereafter it was a book a year for Barry Crump and AH & AW Reed, as the restless author moved himself around New Zealand, mainly in country jobs and places, then croc-hunting in Australia and island-squatting in the Great Barrier Reef. The publishers had a struggle coaxing the annual 50,000 words from the Good Keen Man, when writing interfered with his wandering ways.

After ten books Crump decided to move on. Good as the royalty payments had been, the discipline of publishing a book every year in Wellington had become restrictive. He manoeuvred his way out of his obligations to Reed and shifted base to Auckland.

Alex Hedley, the master bookseller, ordered 1000 copies of *Hang on a Minute Mate* and sold many more than a thousand. Crump caught on as the epitome of the Outdoor Man, and booksellers throughout New Zealand had a bonanza.

After this Alex Fry dropped out of things but I had to write the final chapter of the next book, *One of Us*, because Crump had 'gone bush' and the printers were waiting.

When I ordered simultaneous reprints of 5000 each of *A Good Keen Man* and *Hang on a Minute Mate* the Sydney manufacturers phoned a couple of weeks later to say that they had inadvertently bound the books inside the wrong covers – what to do? My solution was to guillotine the 10,000 books out of their covers and bind them together as a "Crump Special", titled *Two in One*. Reeds sold the lot.

Barry Crump was a major figure in the publishing break-out that Reeds achieved in the 1960s. The other authors who helped create the boom market for New Zealand books included Mona Anderson, Kenneth and Jean Bigwood, Peter McIntyre and Terry McLean.

New Zealand booksellers had never before had a range of bestselling books instantly available on demand, as they were from the Reed warehouses in Wellington, Auckland and Christchurch. The books were virtually risk-free because the demand, before television, was nationwide and the authors were household personalities.

Opportunist writers set out to jump on the Crump bandwagon, but effectively he had no rivals. He was blessed with a keen ear and a yarn-spinner's memory. Given the start-line on a yarn, his imagination drew on his own experiences and those of his mates (which were never dull, embroidered and exaggerated and lubricated as they were). Crump's urge to convince and entertain shaped the raw material into best-selling fiction.

Crump was the greatest non-musical entertainer New Zealand has produced and he embodied and enhanced that role to perfection – the face and the hat, the lean body and its bushman's clobber, and the irresistible grin through which the gravel voice made its way. With a supporting cast of dogs, horses, a vintage vehicle and a succession of female companions, Crump made his personal presence felt throughout New Zealand, a decade before television turned him into an electronic media personality.

His public presence of banter and reminiscence shrouded a hidden, low-key Kiwi, who was only different from the rest of us in his urge to entertain and his compulsion to keep moving on. The sedateness of suburbia was not for him and his books epitomised the country beyond the neon and the restricted speed zone. He was a born storyteller and we are fortunate that he had an ongoing urge to write and to be published. In this era of multi-media diversity and small-screen fantasies we shall never see his equal again.

We were living under the name of Mr and Mrs Havisham (out of Dickens) in a flat in Park Road. Jean [Watson] was working at a printery and I was writing my book. I called it A Good Keen Man. It took me about a month and I was just finishing typing it when two policemen came to interview me about lending my name to a bloke for a car deal he'd lashed on. I was already regarded with deep suspicion by our landlady – there was a part in my book where one of the characters gets the end of the toilet-roll caught in his dressing-gown belt and comes out through a hospital ward with it trailing out behind him. I wanted to see if this would actually work so I went along the hall to the toilet and pulled the toilet paper out the door and round the corner. I was partway up the passage when the landlady came in the front door.

"Mr Havisham!" she called out. "What on earth do you think you're doing with the toilet paper?"

"It's just something I'm writing," I stammered.

"I don't allow writing on the toilet paper, Mr Havisham," she barked. "This is a respectable house, I'll have you know. I'll just thank you to roll it up again and leave it as it was."

Anyway the visit from the policemen was the final straw. She gave us a week's notice . . . I just had time to finish off my book.

I offered it to a publisher, who returned it saying that its publication would be profitable neither to them or me. I offered it to another publisher who wouldn't read it. I sent it to Reeds in Wellington, who wrote back to say they'd like to publish it, if I agreed to go through it with a journalist to knock it into shape. Okay, I said, or words to that effect.

We set off for Wellington in a 1934 Chev we bought for fifteen quid, and it took us three months to get there. Had a fair bit of trouble with that car . . . In the evenings and on weekends Alex and I worked on the Book. He taught me a lot about putting one together. More to it than I'd thought.

– The Life and Times of a Good Keen Man

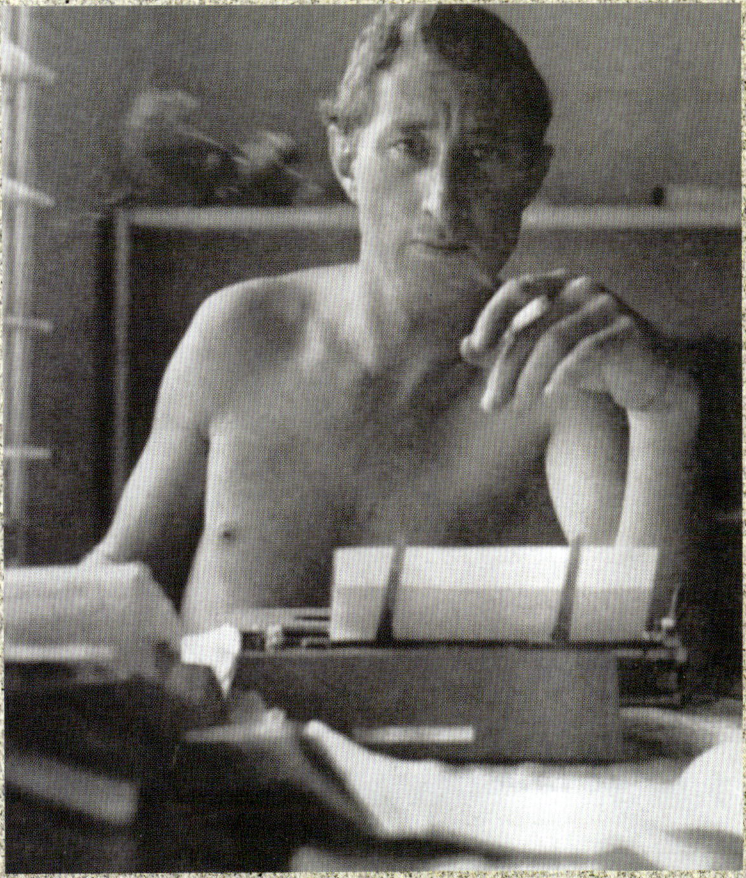

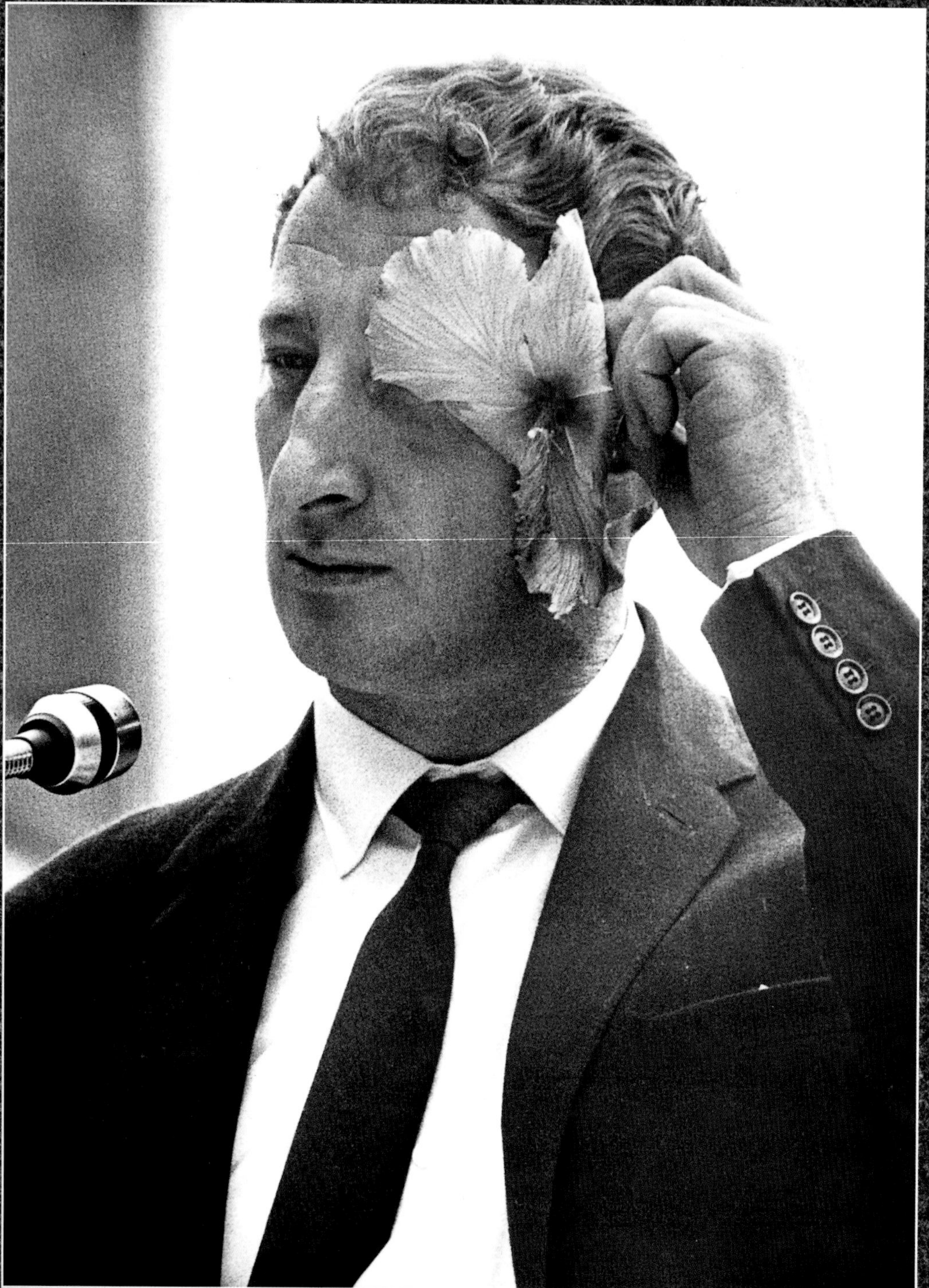

Chapter 3
A Good Keen Girl

I must say . . . I realise how much courage some of my women have had. The smart ones gave up on me early on, but the few that stuck it out hung on through more than you'd expect, just looking at them. I've known plenty of men who'd have chucked it in long before they did. I suppose it's a bit like finding out if a bloke's going to be any good as a deer-culler. You can't tell until you've had 'em out in the scrub for a while.

– The Life and Times of a Good Keen Man

TINA LESTER
(Barry's first wife)

BARRY WAS STRAIGHT OUT OF THE BUSH WHEN WE MET, AND HE WAS QUITE DIFFERENT FROM THE FRIENDS I KNEW. WE MET AT A PARTY AT JOCELYN AND ODO STREWE'S PLACE IN TITIRANGI. HE'D TURNED UP WITH JACK LASENBY, another deerculler he'd met working in the bush. There was a great fashion among deercullers that they never, ever did up their boot laces and in the bush they always wore these nice green swannies with a belt.

As far as Barry starting writing is concerned, Jack Lasenby was very important. Jack was a writer and certainly would have started Barry on his path. Jack could see Barry's potential as a person and as a writer and introduced him to a lot of people. Then Barry and I got together and I introduced him to a lot more. I knew a lot of writers and moved in arty-bohemian circles in those days. It was a very lively, interesting time in Auckland.

When Barry and I first got together we rode around on motorbikes, rock 'n' roll was just in, we got thrown out of the Orange Hall, and the Group Architects were buzzing. Barry had charm and it was fun.

His resourcefulness was extraordinary. He'd lived on his own for a long time doing quite dangerous things. Barry looked good in the bush – I think he was at home there. He had a certain grace of movement and he was amazingly adept. He could make a bed out of teatree saplings; I saw him fashion in five minutes from flax and a nail a most intriguing candle holder that was very useful and quite elegant.

You had to be very strong to survive with Barry. The charm was all there, it was all real. There was this warmth that people warmed their hands at, he made you feel special. They're valuable these people like Barry, they're like the salt in the stew.

We were married no more than three years. It wasn't long but it certainly was vibrant. I gave him confidence, I gave him some sort of security too, although I don't think he needed it. I couldn't understand, and he could never explain, why he was constantly taking off.

We stayed good friends over all the years. I miss him, I liked to know he was there.

Did a winter on pigs and goats at Colville on the Coromandel Peninsula, bought a Norton Dominator motorbike and wound up in Auckland, where one of the shooters introduced me to a woman who I thought was pretty beaut.

I still think so. She must have thought I was a bit beaut too, because we ended up getting married. And then pregnant.

"That'll stop your gallop, Crump," one of my mates remarked.

– The Life and Times of a Good Keen Man

MARTIN CRUMP
(Barry and Tina's son)

The first time I remember meeting my father was on my ninth birthday. My mother, Tina, talked to Barry on the phone and he promised to pick me up for a night out, but my excitement turned to anxiety as the evening wore on and he didn't show up. When he finally arrived at 11 pm he'd brought two cheeseburgers and a hammer. Mum had told him I was interested in carpentry and that was my birthday present

I don't remember being hurt or disappointed. It would have been much worse if he hadn't turned up at all. Although that's the first time I remember meeting Barry, I know now that I had seen him before then, at times quite regularly, but I had somehow forgotten. I'd remember the places and other people that were there, but not my father. I know, for instance, that we visited him in Waihi because I remember the croquet lawn, but I don't have any recollection of Barry.

I do remember seeing Barry on *Town and Around* on television. "That's your Dad," Mum would say, and there he was doing all these crazy things. I was quite proud of him. And of course adults were looking at me and saying, "That's Barry Crump's son." Later that was very difficult. Some people wouldn't have given me the time of day if I was just Martin Lester, but as Barry Crump's son . . . never Martin Crump, always Barry Crump's son.

I wasn't much good at school and left at fourteen. My first job was on a farm, then I got a job at the Joseph Lucas spare parts department. We'd heard very little of Barry. He hadn't written many books and he'd been overseas trying to find God.

One day this guy walks into the spare parts department, hat on, handlebar moustache. I thought, my goodness, he looks familiar. I'm six foot two, fourteen stone and fourteen years of age and he would never have known I'd be that size at that age. I'm staring at him and he's looking over at me and I get the better of him.

"Look," he says, "you've got a lot of guts looking an adult in the eye like that. What's your problem?"

"Your name Barry?"

"Yeah."

"I'm your son, Martin," I say, and shake his hand.

He got all fidgety and "goodness gracious me, boy, what shall we do?" wanting to do the dad bit. We ran around together for a day or two but the dad bit never happened.

I remember feeling nervous when I met Barry. It was more like meeting someone famous than a son meeting his father, and I had that feeling again when we met up in 1981 when I was twenty-one. That was the year I got to know my father.

Barry had just written a book called *Shorty* about a farmer who got golf fever and was so hooked he used to hit balls against the cow shed in the dark so he knew where to find them in the morning. Shorty's fever must have been contagious because it spread to Barry and me.

I introduced him to the Waitakere Golf Club in the ranges west of Auckland. You wouldn't know there's a golf course there. You drive up the gravel road, come over the hill and the bush opens up into a valley. Twenty minutes from Auckland, it was Crump land. He loved the remoteness and he lived on the course after that – literally. He and his wife Robyn parked their VW van there and used the clubhouse for showers and toilets. Because he was short of cash, Barry would write an article for the club magazine to pay for his golf fees.

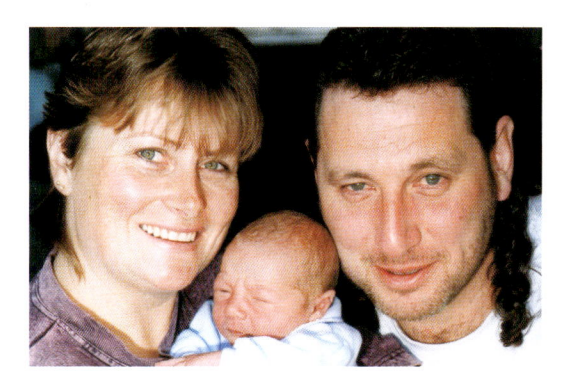

We'd play on Mondays and Tuesdays and sometimes sneak in another game or two on a Wednesday or Sunday. After the first round on Monday we'd stop for Vogels bread sandwiches and a mug of tea, then we'd head off for round number two, which was never as intense as the first one. We'd get a bit tired and the score would start ballooning out. Sometimes we'd completely lose it and start putting each other off. I'd say, "Nice shot, Barry," when he'd only be on his back swing, or he'd throw something at my ball so it would fall off the tee just before I hit it. We didn't like crowds so we avoided weekend golf and didn't play much with other people. We were getting to know each other and having fun doing it.

Barry needed cash so he got himself a job at Radio Pacific as a talkback host with Robyn producing the show. They called it *The Bush Telegraph* and it ended up with quite a following. The beauty of the job was it was 5 am to 7 am, which of course fitted nicely with his new-found passion for golf.

Sometimes we'd stop at the Baha'i place at the back of Henderson and light a fire, and he'd tell me a story or another piece of his life. I just wanted to hear him talk and it was wonderful. Three months into the year we were having a wonderful time. It was like I'd found my best friend as well as my father.

"The big competition's on today, Martie, and I'm going to thrash you mate, matey potata," said Barry. His term of affection was "matey potata". We were looking forward to a game out at Muriwai, a beautiful links course out on the coast. It was a beautiful day, everything was right, we got to about the third hole, it was a par five, far end of the course, I hit my drive okay and all of a sudden the hair rose on the back of my head and I just lost it, I was so angry. It was a red rage, I couldn't see anything, couldn't see the golf course, couldn't focus, I was so angry. I couldn't focus on the anger either, it was blind fury and it came over me like a heart attack.

I took every ball out of my bag, one by one, threw them on the ground and hit them as hard as I could. I had no idea where the golf balls went, but I found one and carried on hitting it. It felt like I'd done something terrible, feeling this anger and acting like I did. I couldn't believe I could ever feel this way – I didn't know I had it in me. We got to about the ninth hole back at the clubhouse with me hitting this one ball and Barry still hadn't said a word. He just carried on and he kept real quiet.

"What are you like at pool?" said Barry.

"I can hold my own."

"Okay," he said, "let's go."

We drove to the Huapai Tavern and of course any time he walks into a place like that everyone's going, "Crumpy, Crumpy," but he said, "No, I've got a vendetta here, my son and I, we've got this match and we can't be interfered with."

We had gin and bitters and DB Export beers, about twenty of those and about as many games of pool to match. Hardly said a word to each other. I was aggressive, anyone dare look at me sideways and I'd be having them. It got to five o'clock and the local workers were coming in and I was crashing into them, just daring them to look or to say one word to me; I was going to have a go, I was so angry.

I know now the anger was about Barry but at the time I didn't have a clue. I was so upset with myself. I loved golf and I loved playing with my father, and I'd blown the beautiful day at Muriwai with this filthy temper I never knew I had. I suppose underneath I'd had this feeling, why couldn't we have had more of this? You bastard, shooting through. Why couldn't I have had a lot more of this, you mongrel?

But it took me years to figure that out and I've done a lot of healing since then. He brought it up years later, not directly about that day but about not being there for us as a father, and it absolutely floored me. I was nearly to the end of telling a story about something that had happened to me, and I said without thinking, it was just a manner of speech, "You should have been there." And he said, "Yeah, you're bloody right, I should have been there."

But he couldn't have been there, for whatever reasons. Okay, he did some dirty things, promising this, that and the other and never making it. A lot of men were like that, he wasn't the only one. He just happened to be who he was and everyone wanted to be part of his life because he was so bloody wonderful to be with when he wanted to be. I know he meant it when he said he loved me or he loved a wife or a girlfriend. At the time he meant it. He was like that, he was intense for a time. And then he'd move on. He didn't want you to get to know him too well because if you did you'd find out about this other side, and I saw that other side, it was the cruel, gutless side. I've been gutless too and I don't like it. In that year I did find out what I had inherited from him.

But it was a wonderful year and we shared all sorts of things. Sometimes we'd visit friends: Bryce Peterson, Paul Bennett and Linda Poulton, the Greaves family – wonderful, talented people, songwriters and singers. I used to sit quietly and listen and strategically place a guitar against a chair. One of them would pick it up and start strumming, then out of nowhere there would be a party.

Sometimes Barry would do the 'Crumpy' thing and tease Robyn about being a rotten housewife because every time he went to piss in the sink it was full of dishes. But when he wasn't trying to entertain me, which I loved as well, he was fitting in with my needs, trying to be a father to his son. This unique quality of Barry's, his ability to fit in with most people, and his intuitive ability to perceive the atmosphere in a room and know what was needed, was what made him a special human being as well as a famous man.

I remember for entertainment on a Sunday we'd sometimes head off to a hotel out by the airport to welcome a bus load of tourists into the country. Barry wasn't a snappy dresser. He'd have his jeans and sneakers and a vinyl jacket on and because his hair was thinning on top he would pat his hair forward with his hand. The truth was that the airport hotel was the only place around town you could get a drink and feed on a Sunday.

Barry worked for me as a waiter once. I was catering and had the contracts for the Franklin Country Club and the Pukekohe Cossie Club. The Franklin Country Club was a gentlemen's club, a little old-fashioned, a little behind the times. I think they'd only just let ladies into the place. We were pretty quiet early into the evening, up until about six or seven o'clock, so if Barry and his best mate Bryce Peterson turned up, Bryce would entertain us. We'd get so caught up listening to the songs we'd forget what we were supposed to be doing. Bryce and Barry would do some waitering and Bryce would help me cook. Barry was pretty rough as a waiter, and he was a shocking cook.

We went up north for a family wedding. It was to take place in an old church with corrugated iron over the windows which flapped in the wind. You could only get to the church by climbing a fence and walking across a paddock. I was surprised Barry made it – he never made it to anything else. He was invited to our wedding but he didn't turn up.

We'd sorted ourselves out a place to stay in a quarry nearby, so about nine o'clock we got back there, lit a fire and Barry started telling stories. It was pitch dark that night, and bloody cold, and there I was, sitting in shorts and a teeshirt and even though I had blankets and clothes in my car I didn't want to break the spell by going to get them. I was absolutely mesmerised by Barry, he had me enthralled.

Every once in a while I'd grab a piece of wood and chuck it on. We hadn't eaten since the afternoon and I was getting ravenous. The only thing we had was pumpkin, which usually I can't stand, but we slung the camp oven over the fire and cooked it and that night it tasted delicious. In spite of the cold and the strange surroundings, I couldn't have felt better.

The experience must have sparked something off in Barry, because a book came out not long afterwards called *Puha Road*, the same name as the road not far from the quarry.

Barry had that talent and that heart knowledge about people, and he could put it into words. I loved that talent of his. We'd be together driving along and just out of nowhere he'd tell me something – it needn't be a yarn or have a great climax to it – but he had a way of doing it which captured everybody.

At the end of our year together, Barry had moved out of the golf course to a flat in Remuera and was making murmurings about leaving Auckland. I didn't mind – we'd seen plenty of each other and I was sure there weren't going to be these great gaps before we saw each other again. I knew I'd be okay to go and see him again in a few months' time, or he'd come up and see me. But that's not the way it turned out. He sabotaged things completely and it was ten years before we met again.

Barry had started his relationship with Toyota and had a shining new ute. He'd been running around in a little Vauxhall Chevette. I was going to sell my station wagon and buy the Chevette off him. It wasn't as if I asked for it – he offered it to me. I had some money so I wasn't worried about how much he'd want for it.

When I sold my car I told Barry I'd buy the Vauxhall. He sounded a bit strange, said he'd spoken to Robyn and they needed a bit more money. I said, "Go ahead, get the best price you can for it," but if it was a reasonable price I'd pay the money, and that I'd pop around on Sunday.

On Sunday he wasn't there. The furniture was gone, the flat was completely cleaned out. We'd spent four or five days a week together for twelve months and there wasn't one stick of furniture left. Was it over the money? Was it the car? I don't think so.

Six months later I'm in Newmarket and see Robyn, Barry's wife of the time. "Martie, how are you?" she says, comes up, arms wide, we give each other a big hug. And there's Barry hiding in a doorway four doors down.

You mongrel, I thought. I wanted to hit him. What're you afraid of me for, I'm your bloody son. Don't you understand, I don't care . . . ? I couldn't believe that he would actually hide from me.

After he shot through I didn't see him again until 1990. I'd been going out with Adele for ten years and she'd never met Barry. He was in Opotiki living with Eileen. I phoned him and said perhaps it was time we got together again, and he suggested we meet at Putaruru.

Barry turned up with a nine-year-old boy who'd driven him all the way from Opotiki. The boy and Barry were the best of friends. We followed that nine-year-old driving all the way back to Opotiki. "It's more nerve wracking for me than it is for him, you know," Barry said.

They were soul mates. I know Barry shared things with him I would have liked to share. But then Barry shot through and left.

I feel like a great weight's been lifted off me since Barry died. It was like a roller coaster, being with someone like Crumpy, the highs are the highest you're ever likely to be and the lows can be the lowest, but it's great to feel all those emotions.

I hadn't spoken to Barry for six years until the Thursday before he died, when out of the blue he phoned me up. That was uncanny. I'm still stunned by Barry's death, I thought he was invincible, but his funeral made for one hell of a family reunion and for a while afterwards I was meeting and talking with brothers, aunties and uncles I'd never met before. Friends came to the funeral from all over the country and shared their stories, as I shared mine, and I was glad for the time I had with Barry so I could understand why they too had felt so special when they were with him.

I must be a bastard to live with, but I hope I've been good value along the way . . . I've had a pretty good innings so far.

– The Life and Times of a Good Keen Man

ANDREW CAMPBELL
(Son of Fleur Adcock – Barry's second wife)

In 1962, at the age of five, I was the proud recipient of a paperback edition of *Little Boy Jesus at Play*. "Presented to Andrew Crump," read the bookplate, "for good attendance. Signed: Richard Easton, Vicar, St Anne's Sunday School, Wellington."

While I still consider myself a reasonable attendee, if not of religious institutions, I haven't been known as a Crump for over thirty years. This temporary change of identity occurred during a brief and turbulent period when my mother, Fleur Adcock, was married to Barry Crump. I'm not sure why I was known as Andrew Crump at Sunday School – perhaps it was because Barry was hoping to adopt me – but within six months I had reverted permanently to being a Campbell.

One of Crump's favourite jokes featured a father who placed his toddler on the mantelpiece, said, "Jump to Daddy," stepped aside as the child crashed to the floor, then added, "That'll teach you, son – never trust anyone." But, despite his occasionally warped sense of humour, Crump was genuinely fond of children. He was nice to me as a child, if not always to my mother, and one of the first things he said when we met up again a quarter of a century later was, "You were a lovely baby, mate."

My memories from those early days are scattered and vague. I can remember throwing confetti over Fleur and Barry as they left the registry office in Wellington. I also recall seeing Crump's rifle hanging on the livingroom wall and fantasising about using it to defend my mother during one of their stormy arguments. Then there was the time I was carried around in the bottom of a sleeping bag slung over Crump's shoulder, before being woken from a deep sleep by my panic-stricken mother, who thought I'd suffocated. The interminable drives in Crump's Land Rover – the notion of driving a Japanese four-wheel-drive would have been unthinkable in those days – have also left their mark, as have equally interminable waits for Barry outside houses, or perhaps public houses.

Other memories are second-hand: my mother creeping to Crump's bedside after a drunken row, about to brain her sleeping husband with a massive Latin dictionary, and his arm shooting out automatically to grab her wrist in mid-descent . . . Crump and his mate drinking a bottle of medicinal ether after the grog had run out . . . my mother falling down some steps and breaking her arm after an altercation with Barry . . . Crump affecting bush credibility by deliberately ripping his jeans before a photo shoot . . .

I'm sure no one was surprised when Barry and Fleur split up. Fleur would have tried hard to be a good keen girl, but they had little in common apart from a love of words – and the words of *Hang on a Minute Mate* were very different from those of her book *The Eye of the Hurricane*. A long-term Anglophile, she demanded one and a half tickets to England (aboard the Fairsea) by way of a separation settlement. He agreed, throwing in his portable typewriter as a gesture of good faith, and we went our separate ways.

I don't remember Crump saying goodbye. I do, however, have a clear recollection of his promise to post me a stuffed crocodile after his next hunting expedition to Australia. For years afterwards, my heartbeat would quicken whenever I saw a postman delivering interesting-shaped parcels to the residents of East Finchley . . . but I remain disappointed to this day.

Twenty years later I returned to New Zealand, and after several false starts I found myself working as managing editor for Reeds, Crump's original publishers – one of those coincidences that New Zealand seems to specialise in. Crump had long since decamped and was now self-publishing his books, which were distributed very profitably by one of our competitors. I'd been thinking about catching up with Crump for some time – my mother had always seemed to look back on their relationship with more amusement than bitterness – and this gave me the excuse I needed: I would fill in a few gaps in my personal history and attempt to lure New Zealand's most popular novelist back to Reeds at the same time.

In those days Crump was living in the backblocks of Opotiki. I had already arranged a holiday in Gisborne, so I decided to stop off at Crump's place on the way, driving a brand-new Toyota Corolla that had come with my job. Crump's directions, elicited over the phone, seemed straightforward enough – "Take the first left south of Opotiki, keep on going to the end of the tar-seal, hang a left, carry on till a creek gets in the way, then lean on your horn till I come and get you," (or words to that effect) – but I'd forgotten that I was dealing with a man who routinely drove up near-vertical hillsides just for the hell of it.

As it turned out, the road was virtually impassable in a 1300 cc Japanese sedan, but by the time I'd realised that, it was too late to turn back. With a sheer drop on one side, impenetrable bush on the other, and deep, water-filled ruts in between, it was the kind of road that would make a hardened rally-driver blanch.

I came within a hair's breadth of writing off the Corolla on its maiden expedition that day. And I'd probably still be there in deepest Opotiki if I hadn't asked my passengers to disembark while I took a desperate flying charge at the last, steepest, muddiest part of the so-called road. Somehow I avoided plummeting down the bank, and none of the parts that fell off the car seemed to prevent it from working. With one last wheel-spinning wallow, I pulled up alongside the creek Crump had referred to, opposite a small collection of buildings that I took to be his farm.

Judging from the amount of horn-sounding required to attract his attention, Crump must have been working on the other side of his property – too far away, I hoped, to have witnessed my embarrassing lack of driving prowess. After twenty minutes or so of frantic honking, I noticed a Toyota Land Cruiser start up outside one of the sheds, bounce across the paddock, work its way down the bank, splash across the creek, climb confidently up the other bank, and come to rest beside its mud-splattered stable mate.

"Andrew – good to see you, mate . . . Jeez, you didn't bring that little car down the four-wheel-drive track, did you? There's a proper road in here, now. You must've been watching too many of those Toyota ads."

Crump looked – and sounded – exactly as I'd imagined. Wearing a swanndri, gumboots and a battered brown hat that bore a remarkable resemblance to the one he'd been wearing the last time I saw him, he told me he'd spent the morning butchering a cow, but hadn't been able to fit it into his freezer. "The dog's had a good feed, anyway," he said, gesturing at the surreal sight of a disembodied cow's head sitting in the paddock.

Crump's home was a tiny shed with a corrugated-iron chimney and an overflowing chest freezer on the front porch. I discovered later that his was the farm's shearing quarters, which he'd moved in to after feeling uncomfortable rattling around in the big house up the hill. In the corner of the main room, a woman was crouched in front of a tiny television, avidly watching a screen that was covered with dancing white specks. I sensed we'd interrupted a row, as she said nothing all afternoon except to complain about the picture, and Crump's conversation was punctuated with sarcastic enquiries about the movie she was attempting to watch.

"I've got ten sons by ten different mothers," Crump announced after making us a brew. "They all come and check me out, but not many of them show up again . . . Still, who can blame them, eh? I've done too much roaming to be much of a dad."

A deep, rumbling sound came from Crump's direction. It took me a moment to realise that he was singing – in a basso profundo – "I was born under a wandering star . . ." It was so unexpected that I had to stifle a laugh.

Strolling around the farm, we chatted about old times, family and friends – but mainly about books. Sargeson, Dylan Thomas and Auden are names that come to mind. Despite his Kiwi joker image, Crump was a man of letters in his own way, and he was just as interested in literature as he was in deerculling or bushcraft. He was also interested in the mechanics of publishing and seemed to enjoy the additional control he'd had over his books since he wrested them away from Reeds. Against the incongruous backdrop of evil-eyed pedigree goats and mauled cow parts, we analysed the

Auckland publishing scene – the petty struggles for power, the infighting, the relentless cycle of mergers, takeovers, restructurings and downsizings . . . perhaps the backdrop wasn't so incongruous after all.

Soon it was time to leave. I wanted to tackle the Waioeka Gorge before nightfall, and there was also the drive back to Opotiki to consider. As we returned to the shed to say goodbye to Crump's friend, who was still trying to make sense of the electronic snowstorm in the corner, I gave Barry a dog-eared photograph of him, Fleur and me, taken in similar surroundings but happier times several decades earlier. He smiled and pinned it on the wall, next to one of him and Scotty.

I didn't make it to Crump's funeral, But if I had, I know what my valediction would have been.

"Where's my bloody crocodile, Crump?"

Then I met and married Fleur, a poet, an academic and librarian. She worked at the Alexander Turnbull Library. It was a turbulent affair, we went through the whole relationship in about five months.

– *The Life and Times of a Good Keen Man*

JEAN WATSON

Jean had an imperturbable contentedness about her. She was happy whatever we were doing, and some of the work was hard. After a good night's hunting [in Australia] we could have ten or a dozen crocs to skin and scrape and pack in salt. They're tougher to skin than a big stag's neck in the roar and harder still to scrape the meat and fat off, even the small ones, and Jean scraped her share of them.

Most days we'd finish the skins and flop in the shade and sleep the rest of the afternoon under mosquito nets. In the evening we'd wake and eat and paddle off in our little boat, raking the river with our light for the red blaze of crocodiles' eyes. And Jean pulled her weight with everything we did. Good value to have around.

Jean, a psychology student and delicate intellectual flower from the academic fringes of Auckland, quoting T.S. Elliot at poetry-readings and scrawling notes on paper serviettes for a short story she was writing about smells in coffee-bars – [ended up] staggering down the Paringa riverbed in front of me in the rain, the blood from the stag she was carrying dripping down the backs of her skinny legs; clinging to the saddle, only her head and the horse's visible above the water as they got swept down the flooded Mahitahi and only just made it across; holding the harpoon for me as we paddle through a mangrove swamp at night in a cloud of mosquitoes, hundreds of miles from the nearest human habitation, looking for bigger crocodiles; sitting in the hatchway of the Waterwitch beside me in a screaming gale and thirty-foot waves, unable to turn aside until the storm subsided or we went up on the reef; standing on a washed-up log looking for boats when she knew bloody well that no boats were going to come and we were all going to die.

And after years of that she ups and off into the Red Heart of Australia with a bunch of strangers to look for Lassitter's Lost Reef. And all the gutsy things in between.

I hung around Auckland for a while, not knowing what I wanted to do next. Then I met Jean [Watson], a quite remarkable lady. She was a part-time psychology student. We lived in flats around Auckland and both worked. And sat round in coffee bars being intellectuals. At one stage we lived in a converted lifeboat moored to the sewer-line in Hobson's Bay and spent our last ten bob on incense and guitar-strings . . .

~ *The Life and Times of a Good Keen Man*

VANDA LYNDON
(BARRY'S THIRD WIFE)

I was getting bored with city life and moved away to the Bay of Plenty, but just before I left a young lady came around to my flat and told me she was three months pregnant. And it was me. And her old man came up from the South Island to say, "What are you going to do about it, Sport?"

I took her with me and we lived in a cottage in Te Teko and got to love one another (we didn't mind each other in the first place), got married and had two sons. I also assembled a pack of dogs and got back into hunting and fishing and jet-boating and guiding tourists. When we were living there I wrote and recorded a song called "Bad Blue". As songs go it was no hit, but it's a good thing to have done.

After two years at Te Teko we moved to Waihi, where I trapped possums and wrote. Life was easy. Too easy. I'd been getting bored with being successful. It sure had its points but it hadn't answered any of my questions. Even a new station-wagon was a sterile pleasure. There had to be more to life than this. We surely weren't on this planet just to hassle each other for money and die. I was restless.

I wrote a book and had it printed and published it myself, as much for the challenge of it as anything else. This one was entitled *Bastards I Have Met*. It sold out in two weeks and for the first time in my life I had some real cash in my kick.

My wife and I and the two kids stuck ourselves on a passenger-liner to England, where we stayed in London with my good friend Kevin [Ireland]; who was working on the *Times* newspaper. I liked London . . .

—The Life and Times of a Good Keen Man

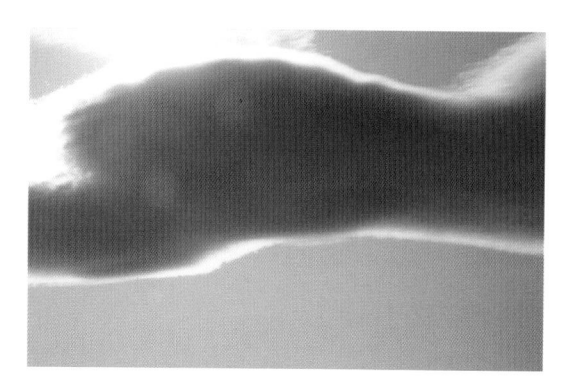

SIMONE RAINGER
(DAUGHTER OF BARRY'S GIRLFRIEND, LENNA)

I WAS FOUR WHEN I FIRST MET BARRY. HE WAS THE BIGGEST PERSON I'D EVER SEEN. HE HAD A PRESENCE I'D NOT SEEN BEFORE – A STRENGTH. I REMEMBER OUR FIRST MEETING VIVIDLY. I WAS SITTING CROSS-LEGGED ON THE LOUNGE FLOOR when mum walked in with Barry and said, "I'd like you to meet Mr Crump." I remember looking up for what seemed an awfully long way and thinking, *'Oh my God – we're in for it!'*

Well, we were in for a lot of things. Firm discipline and fun were top of the agenda. My sister didn't hit it off too well with him. She didn't like strong discipline I think, however my brother and I got on superbly well with him. He was brilliant with me – strict, loving and affectionate. Barry stuck up for my brother at St Michaels Primary School on a number of occasions and many years later they did a stint in the bush together.

Barry played father role, really. He built stilts, tree-huts, and trolleys, took us to the latest James Bond movies and taught me how to play chess when I was all of five years old – a patient man! Quite often, Martin, myself and my brother and sister would go to the Pt Chev picture theatre, eat icecreams and roll jaffas down the wooden floor. Barry believed that he should care for the children he was with and he figured others were caring for his. He was a good wholesome father figure and I will be forever grateful to him for the time he gave to me.

Barry and I had this game together – it began when I was four and never finished. "Touched you last" was the name of the game. He'd come up and touch me with one finger on the leg or shoulder and say "touched you last". Neither of us was allowed to run, so there was no point touching him back then and there. We had to always catch each other unawares. He used to cheese me off because he'd always get me when it was the farthest thing from my mind – like at the dinner table or when he was talking with someone. He could always read me but it was sometimes hard to fathom him. He was an enigma in some ways.

Barry introduced family group meetings every Tuesday night. That was when we had to air our differences if there was something that bugged us. We'd sit there and sit there and if he knew something was up he'd wait until we came out with it. Diplomacy wasn't really taught, it was more like, "Come on, get straight out with it, let's tackle it." You didn't beat around the bush. If it was indirect he corrected it so we were more straightforward. I appreciated that very much. However, this training has probably got me into a bit of strife, too.

Our relationship was open, no secrets – he wasn't that sort of person. But he never aired any dirty laundry either. If there was any rubbish that went on between him and his wives, he never wrote about it in his books or talked about it, never. It was between them and they had to sort it out. He never ran people down. "Oh, I'm not that keen on that bloke," was all he'd say, or "I could never warm to her" – he'd never give you a reason. From my point of view it was a very easy relationship. He only ever whacked me twice, once when I'd gone to my friend's place when I wasn't allowed and the other time was when I'd been repeatedly mucking around with my food – he gave me a good whack on the backside for that. In retrospect, both times were justified and I quickly learnt that when Barry said something you neither questioned him nor argued with him, you just obeyed him – simple.

Mum would often wake us in the dead of night and say, "Quick, Barry wants to go bush," and we'd know to get up immediately, otherwise we'd miss out. I can't remember ever being left behind but I knew if we weren't out that door and in that Land Rover before Barry was we would be. Punctuality was very important to Barry.

Barry's idea of camping with the kids was us three kids sleeping in a pup tent and Mum and Barry in the Land Rover with a tarpaulin or a bit of plastic sheeting rigged up over their legs. We did a fair bit of that, all around the central North Island in the bush, not coastal areas, but lake, stream and river areas.

I don't remember him as a big story teller. We *created* the stories. And I don't remember seeing him writing. But I think he used to write when he went bush. He had a portable typewriter that he would carry around. Mum remembers him writing, always longhand, the little notes he put at the side to fix things, things to go back on that he wasn't that happy about or punctuation correction.

I don't think Mum had any great disagreements with Barry's way of doing things though they did argue about other issues. I think the good part outweighed the unpredictable. They were very happy together. Two weeks of every six he'd be off somewhere – not because they'd had a row, it was more like a cycle. He'd be really lovely for two weeks and then not so good and then absolute hell and slowly everything would be shifted out, and then two weeks later everything would be shifted back in again. He'd go bush or take off to Grafton Road to his flat where Tim Shadbolt sometimes bunked.

We were probably living with him for about three years but he was still around after that. We saw him once or twice at Waihi. In the early seventies we moved back to Parnell from Greymouth and he was soon with Mum again. However, Mum had become a Baha'i and would not live with Barry so he used to stay in his van down at Judges Bay. Mum had remarried and separated in between times and we had a beautiful baby sister whom Barry carted with great ease everywhere he went. He called her 'Milana pyjamas'.

We never wrote, but kept in touch. We'd see each other at Baha'i gatherings, for example. We saw each other a lot in the early seventies and then there was a very big gap between probably 1980 and 1990, the Robyn time, when I had no contact. However, I'd see him and Robyn in Auckland sometimes. I remember seeing him in 1981 shortly after my son, Nicholas, had heart surgery. I'd been through a terribly traumatic time and Barry just looked at me (the way he used to) that special way and I burst into tears.

I never had to stay strong for Barry – I could always be myself. There was an unconditional love, it didn't matter if I'd done something stupid or I was nervous or being ridiculously funny – he was never critical and was often comforting.

I spent a lot of time with Barry in 1992 when he lived in Auckland. This is where I met Maggie, and I later spent a couple of days with them in

Havelock in January 1995, though Maggie and I had seen each other in between times. I didn't get to Tauranga till five weeks before he died. It was the first time I'd been there, and Maggie had sent Barry down to the end of the driveway to meet me. He flashed his lights. I pulled in beside him and we looked at each other for quite a while. It seemed like a couple of minutes but it probably wasn't anything like that. There's that look again, I thought, as we just watched each other.

I followed him up to the house and we had a wonderful evening together. I stayed the night and in the morning when I left Barry was up digging some trenches for drainage. He looked grey in the face, as if his skin was plastered with makeup. It was a misty morning, and Barry said he wished I could see the view. It was, he said, the most beautiful view in the world. Barry had an intense appreciation of nature, so that any natural place was the most beautiful. I thought then that I should take a photograph of Barry and Maggie at Welcome Bay. My camera was in the car, but my head got the better of my intuition and I thought there would be a next time. That was the last occasion I spoke with Barry.

ROBIN LEE ROBINSON
(BARRY'S FOURTH WIFE)

Our first real camp was situated at the head of the Copland Pass. "Our life is a bloody fairy-tale," Crump had told the reporter. "We are happy away from the rat race."

Barry introduced me to many bush skills. There was the supplejack candle holder with its cover made from a bottomless glass bottle, torches made from tin cans with candles. Later, when I was a Brownie leader, I employed some of these almost lost arts and, although Barry never had any children to me, the knowledge has been passed down nevertheless. There were everyday handyman skills he brought into our marriage too. Barry was an immensely practical man.

"Don't moan that I never built you a house," announced Barry proudly as he put the finishing touches on an old makeshift shelter, and indeed it was a work of art. About the size of a regular toilet, it consisted of an old wood stove and chimney fashioned from tin and saplings. The materials were gathered from the remains of an ancient dwelling he'd stumbled across in the bush. The rest he cut down himself. Windowless, it nevertheless boasted a sacking door, so now there was somewhere to cook when it rained and a warm but insecure place for me to wait while he was detained late at night in the township – with the bedroom, the truck! Other husbands might stay out late but at least their wives could go to bed. Not me.

Still, I had no complaints, and everyone told me how contented I was, living such an adventurous lifestyle. It's a shame I never had a camera to send a snapshot to my grandmother in Christchurch, who'd have been so proud I could marry a man who could take care of me.

The time for testing had arrived. I knew I was still on trial. He proposed setting a first possum line up an extraordinarily steep ridge. Test Number One consisted of just getting across a glacier-fed river without being swept downstream. Naturally this meant spending the rest of the day soaked to the waist, but it was a fine winter's morning and the frost was thawing. He had, I was forewarned, a great heart and lungs, "organs that would never let him down". No chick could possibly be expected to keep up, but he promised to be patient with this mere slip of a girl, and a city slicker at that.

He was yet to learn about the reserves of vitality I rarely get a chance to use, and I was not only going to keep up, but out-walk him as well! I called out over the roaring river, "I hope I don't hold you up too much." We started the ascent.

"You all right, honey?" he called back, puffing, beads of perspiration appearing on his brow. "Want a rest?"

I walked reverently behind. "No, of course not. Do you?" replied someone exactly half his age who had controlled breathing down to a fine art.

"Do you always examine the function of a function?" he complained.

"In any subject you care to name," I replied.

Up we went until he could stand it no longer. I removed my pack and continued standing while he sprawled. "You're pretty fit," he said. He had a new look in his eye, respect even. It was certainly the closest he had ever ventured to admitting he was impressed, apart from the time I actually carried him, pack and all, across a river without dropping him in it.

"I didn't know you had real guts," Barry explained. "You're a real bushman."

I ran into one of the Bahais in the street in Greymouth and she told me that they were having a birthday party for Robyn at their house that night.

I went and about an hour after I arrived we loaded Robyn's trailbike and gear into the Model-A and took off down State Highway Six on an adventure that was to last for twelve years. Robyn was just twenty-one and I was forty-three . . .

Going off with an old broke bushman and living in the open and sleeping in the back of a Model-A, in winter, in Rough Creek . . . Carrying me across the creek to save me getting my feet wet and prove she can do it . . . and off round her traps in a pair of high-heeled boots we'd found in the Hokitika rubbish-tip because we couldn't buy her any boots until we sold some skins.

Then three months down the Black River without seeing a house or shop or a road or another woman. That'd rock most people. Whited-out in a snow storm on our trapline in Otago prodding ahead with a stick because the edge is just over there somewhere and if we don't find the track down we'll die up here . . . Robyn never jibbed at anything and she never complained. The only thing I knew her to give up on was me, and I don't blame her for that.

– The Life and Times of a Good Keen Man

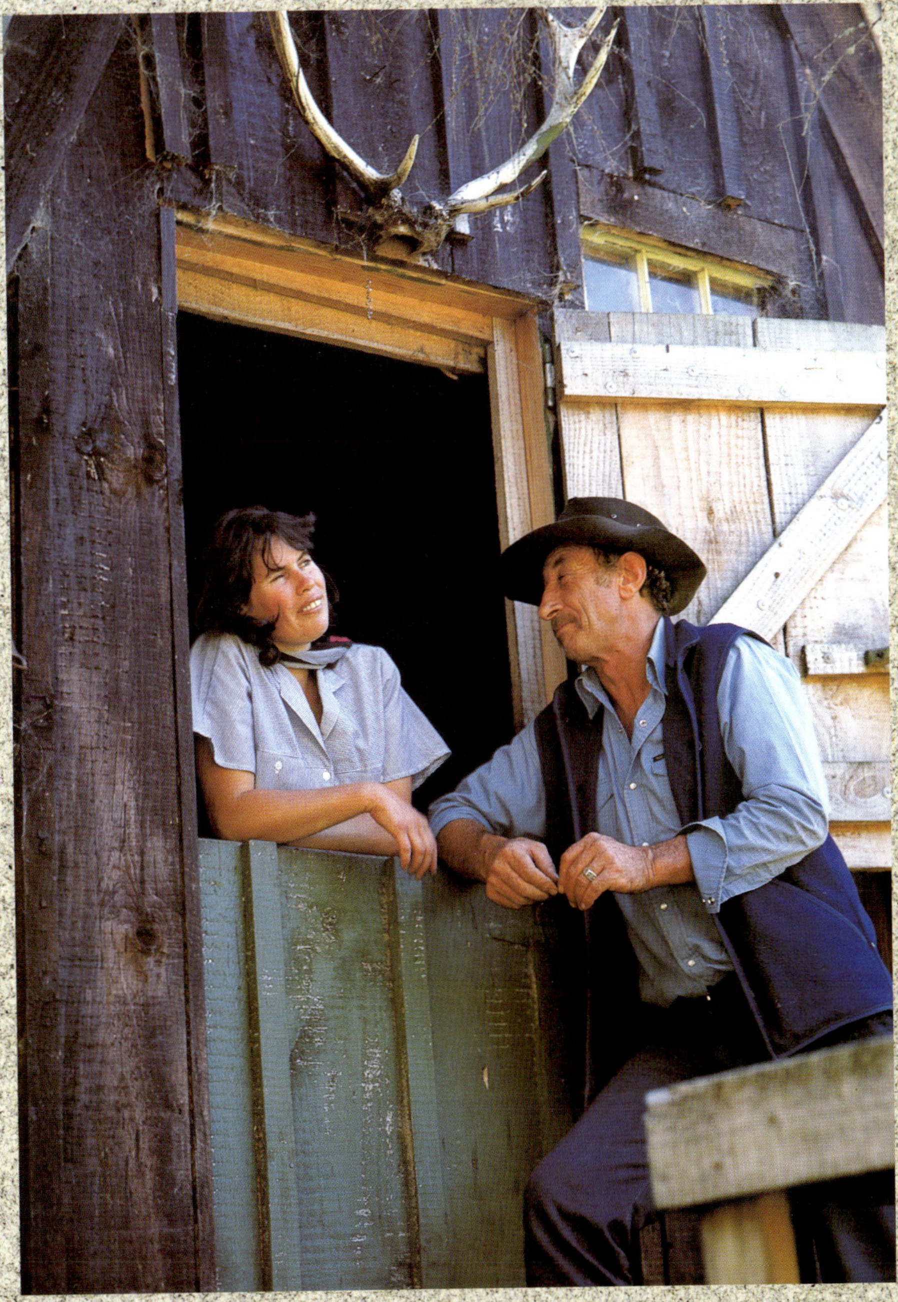

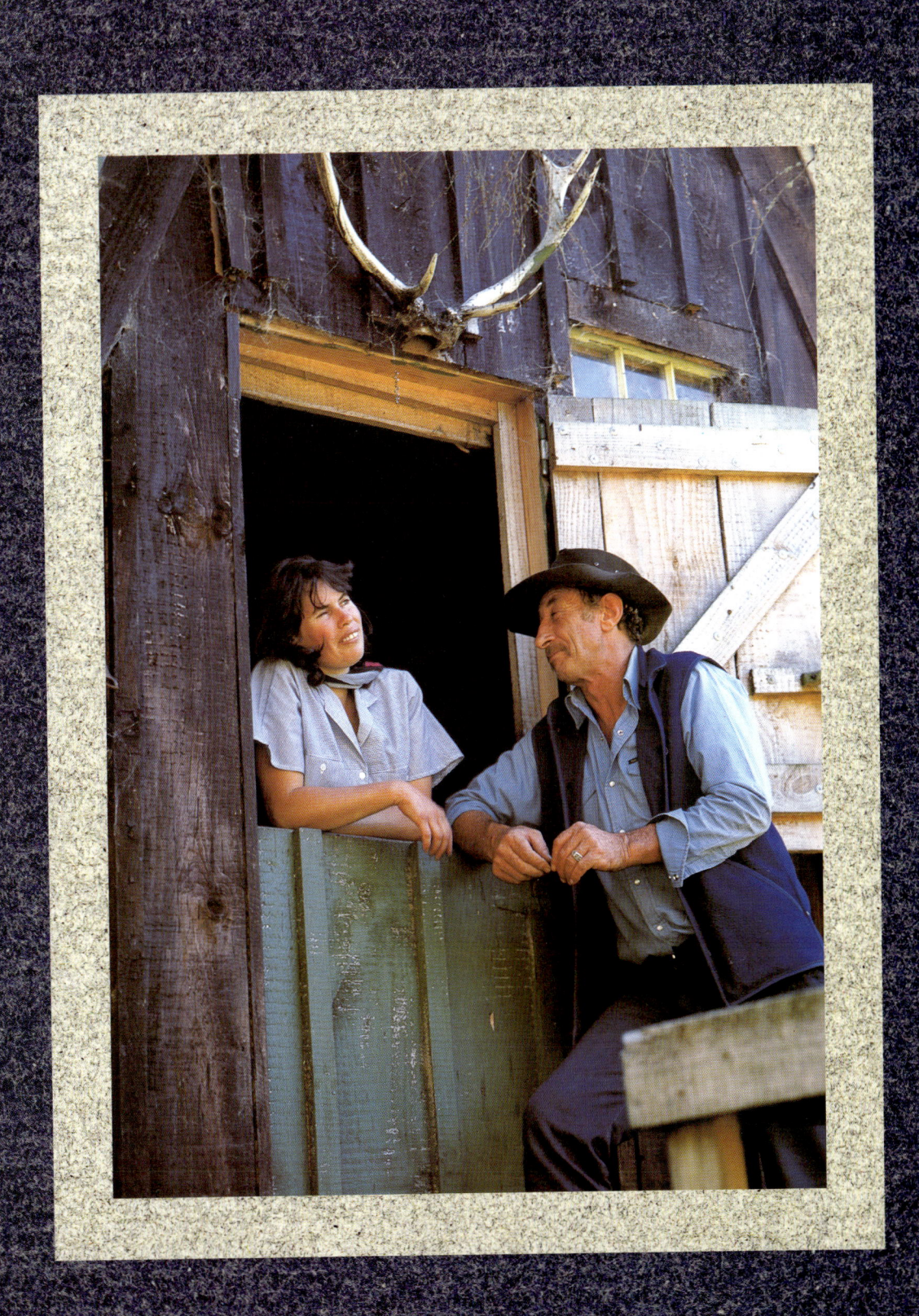

MAGGIE CRUMP
(Barry's Widow)

I'm sitting at the kitchen table on a drizzly, dull Wednesday morning. Anton has left for school and the animals have all been fed — goats, chickens, doves, lambs, geese, cats and a dog. The day is now mine.

During the past few weeks I've been reflecting on the four years I spent with Crumpy and how they have changed my life and direction. Prior to this I was living in suburbia Auckland working nine to five. To supplement my income and support a hefty mortgage I accommodated home-stay students. I was also the mother of four boys and, although three of them were in their late teens, I had a five-year-old who was totally dependent on me. The pace was hectic but it was all I knew. I had a close network of friends and family. I was independent, happy and surviving.

It seems fate had alternative plans mapped out for me. One day out of the blue my orderly, routine world was picked up and tossed into a whirlwind of change, activity, disorder, exhilaration, chaos, bewilderment and excitement. I met and fell in love with a man called 'Crumpy', a Kiwi bushman and novelist. A man who cut his hair by the flame of a 'Bic' lighter. A man who reckoned two shirts was one too many. A man who could pack up all his worldly possessions in the space of 20 minutes. A man who taught me the magic of candlelight. A man who was a stranger to the micro-chip. A man who taught me to cook in a cast-iron camp oven. A man who understood and loved others for their frailties. A man who introduced me to Baha'i. A man who fell in love with a city girl. A man who said,

"Don't hunt for deer in pig country."

One day Crumpy asked me to leave Auckland with him and putting aside a home filled with Queen Anne furniture and the security of familiar faces and surroundings I hopped aboard a Hilux with a five-year-old son and a few battered suitcases. Friends and family from both camps gave us a few months to sort out the infatuation. We were an impossible combination, they believed – worlds too far apart.

I asked him one day, "Why me?" I believed he could have had the pick of any woman he chose. His reply, "How many women do you know who would have the guts to leave everything behind and take off into the unknown?" Looking back, he was right. I couldn't think of one I knew who would have taken up such an incredible challenge. Some may view this as irresponsible, reckless and impulsive, others as adventuresome and gutsy, but whatever it was, I'm glad I took it on. No regrets.

And so Crumpy and I settled in Wanaka for a couple of years and I was introduced to a rural environment. We lived a humble existence and I learnt to live and enjoy life without my shawl of material comforts. We mixed with musterers, shearers and high-country station owners. The great and the small were all the same to him. We rode horses and shot rabbits, gold-panned, watched our son play rugby, entertained television crews, got married, wined and dined with the Toyota network, attended Government House, judged a dog barking competition and wrote and typed books. We survived the odds.

From Central Otago we went to Marlborough Sounds and a home on a 55-foot fishing boat. Pelorus Sound was our home for a time. It was the last piece of this country that hadn't been explored by our Good Keen Man. He loved the simple lifestyle and lack of materialistic encumbrances of its inhabitants. The beauty and enchantment of this isolated spot held its own magic.

But our final resting place together was in a piece of this country that Crumpy always said had it all, and is aptly named the Bay of Plenty. Tucked away in the hills behind Tauranga we found it for what was but a short time.

Throughout our time together Crumpy pushed me to limits I didn't realise I was capable of achieving. He awakened in me strengths and opened horizons that will remain with me for the rest of my life. He was an incredible part of my life, a man so talented, wise, humble, caring, spiritual and yet weary and perhaps out of step with today's time.

And now this bird with a broken wing has to learn to fly again. Perhaps his final challenge for me. I'll take it up just as I did four years ago. A deer he found in pig country. But I've got the last say – "Our goats are getting out of your 'goat-proof fences', so we're quits my darling!"

JETHRO CRUMP
(BARRY'S STEPSON)

I RECEIVED A PHONE CALL FROM MUM ONE NIGHT WHEN I WAS STILL LIVING IN TAURANGA AND ATTENDING TAURANGA BOYS' COLLEGE. MUM HAD BEEN TO LUNCH ONE DAY IN QUEEN STREET, AUCKLAND, WITH SOME OF THE MANAGEMENT from Housing Corporation. Anyway, she told me they were all having lunch and "who should walk through the door with his manager but Barry Crump". So, being the cheeky person Maggie is, she shouted out, "Crumpy, where's Scotty?" and he replied "On the back of the Hilux, Honey." I couldn't believe she had made such a ridiculous call. I was at the other end of the phone shaking my head. He then sat down with them and they started talking. It turned out that he needed a typist for his latest book and so, being the eager beaver my Mum was, she piped up jokingly, "I'll do it for a thousand dollars," and he replied "Okay". So here I was sitting on the other end of the phone listening to how this humorous, keen Auckland secretary had obtained an important job for one of New Zealand's most well-known and famous personalities.

I got off the phone and I was really excited. However, two weeks later I was in Auckland with my brother Simon and some friends, and Mum said, "Do you boys want to meet Barry Crump?" My mates and I were pretty much trembling at the knees. A quick phone call, and there we were cruising into town to have a chitchat with Crumpy. He lived in this apartment attached to a massive warehouse, just off Queen Street. We arrived and beeped the buzzer then went in.

The first thing I saw was the most wicked-looking Hilux, and I thought, shit, this must be Barry's place. We cautiously ventured up the stairs into the apartment and he stood up and introduced himself. I think he was a bit taken by these five boys who all stood staring at him.

Mum continued seeing Crumpy and it developed into a relationship. Word also got out at home that our mum was going out with Barry Crump. All these keen kids would come up and say, "Is your mum scoring Crumpy?" I remember one day I was staying at my mate's house and his mum starting asking me all these questions such as, "Has he got a single brother?" School ended so we spent the summer holidays cruising around with him. We went out in the Marlborough Sounds in his boat and spent New Year far up north

at Stoney Bay. The whole time I couldn't get over how famous he is. Anywhere we went the whole crowd would stop and stare. People at traffic lights would get out of their cars wanting autographs. We would get photographed when we went out to restaurants.

Anyway, the summer finally came to an end. Crumpy and Maggie decided they wanted to make an adventurous trip sightseeing around the South Island. I had got into King's College through Crumpy's name and a bit of rugby formalities, so was off to boarding school.

Just before they went on one of their many great adventures, Crumpy was dropping me off at school, and at that time all the TV cameras were at King's, filming the King's College *Tuesday Documentary*. We had just pulled in to the gates and we were instantly surrounded by cameras and interviewed. We finished the interview with Crump doing a big wheelie in the Hilux on the prestigious King's College rugby field in front of the film cameras. As I was walking off to my boarding house, I thought "What the hell has my crazy mother got us into?"

SIMON CRUMP
(Barry's Stepson)

My days with Crumpy and Mum in Wanaka, I can honestly say, were the craziest that I have experienced. There were many ups and downs with the two of them and my little brother, Anton, but I'm not going to talk about the downers because everyone has them and no one wants to dwell on them. I'm going to talk about the good times and there were plenty of those. There was lots of laughter in the home.

In Wanaka I attended Mt Aspiring College. Crumpy and Mum sometimes picked me up from school. One particular afternoon they thought it would be a bit entertaining to park and wait for me in a different location. They chose the top of the hill across the road from the school and in view of all the pupils who came out of the gate. No one could mistake Crumpy's Hilux. So you can imagine the nice shade of pink I turned as I had to trip up the hill and climb into the Hilux with all my mates staring and yahooing. But the thing is that it didn't satisfy them doing it just the once. Once a week they managed it, sometimes twice and if I was very lucky three times just to keep me on my toes.

Another memorable occasion occurred in my sixth form English class at Mt Aspiring. It all began when we had to hand in a short story on a subject of our choosing. We had a few days to complete this assignment but I ran out of time. The night before the due date I told the olds what I had to achieve by next English class. I got a ticking off by Crumpy for leaving things to the last minute and then he went and rummaged around in a box that held a lot of his writing and produced a story that he had written a few years back that had never ever been published. "Here," he said, "this'll get you top marks. Might be your start to fame." I got Mum to type it up on the computer and very proudly I handed in my work of art by New Zealand's top author. A few days passed and I received my marked masterpiece back. The olds, by this time, were pretty keen to know what top mark I had been given. I got a mark all right, a big fat 'D'. Lowest in the class. Well all hell broke loose when I relayed this to Crumpy and it took some very fast talking by Mum and me to stop him marching up to the school and confronting my English teacher about her ability to teach! Afterwards we had a great laugh about it and Crumpy took great delight in recalling the incident and relating it to people.

Then there was the time when I was dragged out of bed and introduced to twenty-five armed offenders squad members who had frequented our home for a party. They were in Wanaka for a Police fun-run raising money for a cancer charity and Crumpy had met a few of them in the local pub the day before their run. Apparently he had mentioned to them that if they were hard up for something to do that evening they could drop in home. Around 10 pm vans and cars pulled into the driveway and out they poured. It was a great night. One of the guys was about six foot five inches tall and well into the night he had had a few too many beers and he began to eat the moths that were flittering around our light bulb in the lounge. Handfuls of them were disappearing into his mouth. The room was in hysterics.

The next day they came back and collected Crumpy and me and took us to a target shooting spot. It was hard case to be surrounded by cop cars and armed offenders and to watch them blasting holes the size of tennis balls into blocks of wood. We were given a chance to prove our skill, which was a real buzz – a great time and a great memory.

And the last, but not least, of my memories with Crumpy was a time when I was down with the musterers in the sheep yards getting the sheep ready for drenching. The old boy had just received a new Hilux from Toyota

and he was giving it a paddock test run, and what better place and time than when all the musterers could watch the event. He came blasting into the paddock at top speed. Unfortunately it was winter and a few of the puddles had iced up. He came straight towards the fence and then applied the brakes for a speedy turn, skidded on ice and hit the fence. A bit of paint was scratched and an amused bunch of musterers witnessed that one. Crumpy took it all in his stride with his head out the window and a sheepish grin, followed by, "Amazing what these things'll do."

There was never a dull moment when he was around. You never knew what was going to happen next.

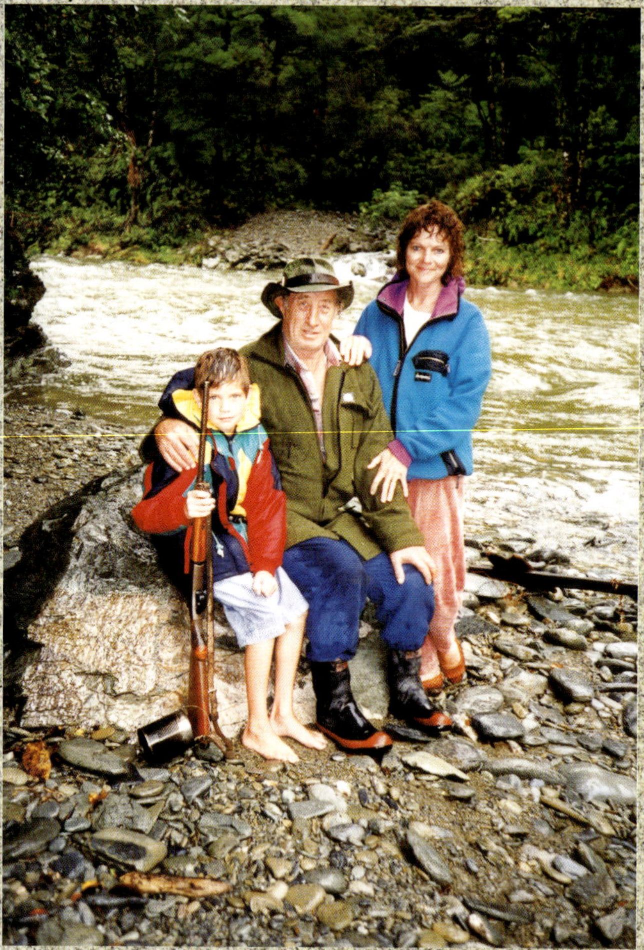

ANTON CRUMP
(Barry's Stepson)

I HAVE A LOT OF MEMORIES OF CRUMPY. MOST OF THEM ARE GOOD ONES. THERE WAS THE TIME WHEN HE LET ME DRIVE OUR NEW BOAT *Punga One.* I WAS SO BUSY CONCENTRATING ON WHERE I WAS GOING THAT I CRASHED INTO A PIECE OF driftwood. He was not too happy about that. But I learnt to drive it real good and sometimes when he was too tired I would drive the boat most of the way back to Havelock from out in the Pelorus Sounds. He kept a good watch but I think he thought I was getting pretty good.

Crumpy taught me lots of things but best of all he taught me this little prayer:

O God, Guide me, protect me, make of me a shining lamp and a brilliant star. Thou art the Mighty and the Powerful. 'Abdu'l-Baha.

STEW NICHOLSON
(BROTHER-IN-LAW)

I was invited to lunch at the Queens Head in Auckland one Friday. My sister Maggie had rung to say she was putting in a few days' typing for Barry Crump on his latest book. She told me to come in and meet him and have a beer. "OK, why not," I said.

Crump looked just as I thought he would. Bush shirt, hat and big grin. "How are you, mate. Maggie's told me a thing or two about you! Ha ha."

"Nothing derogatory I hope," I said looking sheepishly at Maggie. (What the hell's she been telling him, I thought.)

"Nothing," butts in Maggie. "Nothing at all. Don't listen to him, he's just having you on."

The afternoon disappeared discussing how his latest book should end and after twenty rounds at twenty-five dollars it was my shout again, but I had run out of the necessary folding stuff, so told Crumpy it was about time the bar shouted. He remarked that you would be hard-pressed to get anything out of them. The barman didn't agree with my theory either, he reckoned it was more than his job was worth. So I said, call the proprietor we'll have it out with him. I explained the situation to him and fortunately for me he agreed that on this occasion the bar would shout, but don't make a habit of it. I don't know whether he meant spending five hundred dollars on an afternoon's drinking session or asking for a free round!

The dialogue for the ending of Crumpy's latest book was complete, Maggie had disappeared, presumably to type it up. It was now after five o'clock. I told Crump it was the last time I would have lunch with him. He only had to walk to Airedale Street to get home. I had to drive to Ellerslie. He said, "She'll be right, mate, just follow the car in front. You'll be as right as rain," as he swaggered out the door and disappeared down the street.

One year we spent Christmas at Sandy Bay, top of the Coromandel. Crumpy came out in the tinnie with me to set a net. On arrival at the reef we found one oar missing. A few waves over the bow and a foot of water in the boat, and he vowed and declared he'd never go to sea with me ever again. The next morning at daylight I headed out to pick up the kahawai, thirty odd, and an hour later a lone figure on the beach helped me pull the boat in. "Why the hell didn't you wake me up, mate?" A few tips on smoking fish and a little later we had a great feed. Crumpy loved his kai moana.

Looking back, I think he knew his time was up in this life. It seems that so often you just get to know a special friend and they have to leave in one way or another. Crumpy was one of those. Underneath the rough exterior of Crumpy was a big softie, once you got to know him. I found him to be a very spiritual person in a quiet way. One day he handed me a book and said, "Have a read of this when you get a few spare minutes, mate." It was the book of Baha'i.

As a river runs deep, the leaves and bugs floating slowly by, so it was with Crumpy.

Crumpy, you may have cut your load and split this scene but we'll catch up with you, just you wait and see. So tall poppy, 'til we meet again just hang in there. We're thinking of you.

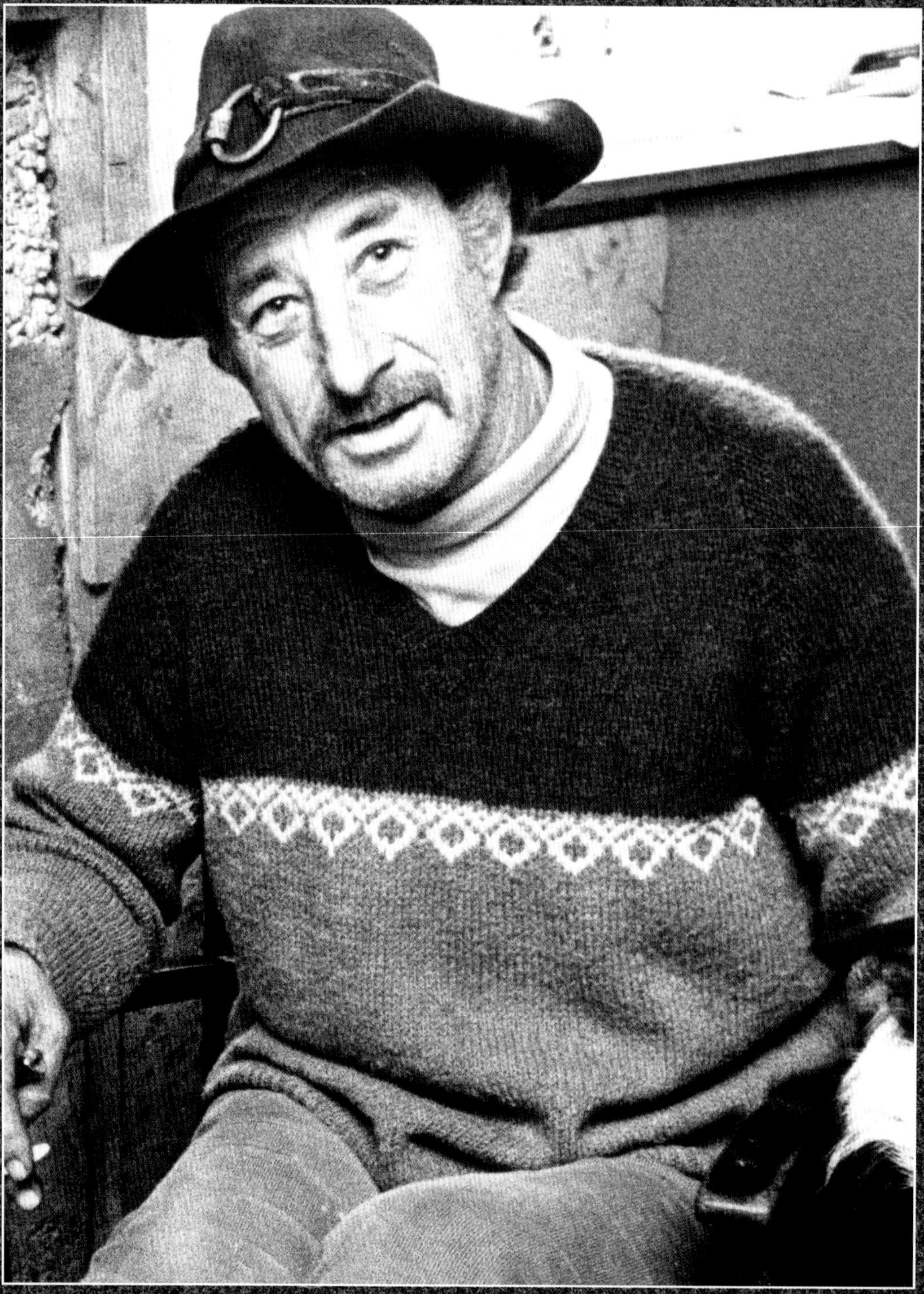

Chapter 4
Bastards I Have Met

ANYWAY, I'VE NEVER MET A BASTARD YET WHO HAD AN ACCURATE IDEA OF HIS OWN B-RATING, AND I DON'T SUPPOSE I'M ANY DIFFERENT FROM ANY OTHER BASTARD. THE SUREST WAY OF FINDING OUT WOULD BE TO ASK SOMEONE WHO KNOWS ME, AND HE'LL TELL YOU, INSTANTLY AND ACCURATELY, PRECISELY WHAT SORT OF BASTARD I AM . . .

WHICH JUST GOES TO SHOW THAT IF WE KNEW AS MUCH ABOUT OURSELVES AS WE CLAIM TO KNOW ABOUT OTHER PEOPLE THERE'D BE MORE SPLENDID BASTARDS LIKE YOU AND ME AROUND.

– Bastards I Have Met

GEORGE JOHNSTON
(Fellow Hunter)

H E CAME INTO AND WENT OUT OF PEOPLE'S LIVES LIKE THEY HAD DREAMT IT, BUT HIS CLOSEST FRIENDS KNEW BARRY WAS ALWAYS THERE IF THEY NEEDED HIM. I WAS A FRIEND OF CRUMP'S FOR THIRTY YEARS AND I BELIEVE I WAS one of the few people who really knew him. At least, that's what he said.

Real friends don't just happen, they develop from a depth of knowledge of each other that requires no explanation. As Crumpy said, all he required of a friend was that his heart was in the right place. That was the deep-thinking Crump that looked beyond the material life that most people find to be all-important.

Our friendship started when Crumpy came down to where I lived in Te Teko, near Whakatane, to do some filming for *Town and Around*. I had a safari business for nearly twenty years, taking clients hunting, shooting and fishing, and also was involved in deer farming and processing. The mid sixties were the early days of television here and camera crews were as rare as rocking-horse shit. We did a lot of filming around the North Island, mostly in the Bay of Plenty and East Coast, for *Town and Around*, and some of them were tremendously funny.

One Sunday in Auckland we ran into a guy from the ad agency which had the British Leyland account and they had to produce a commercial for Land Rover within three days or they'd lose the account. We said we'd do it. Barry took the role of producer and I was the driver. We got a brand-new Land Rover on the Monday morning and then we had to find a cameraman.

"I know just the man for the job," said Crumpy, but when we went around to get him, the guy said he couldn't do the job because he'd pawned his camera. Crumpy got the camera out of hock, we told him what we could do with the vehicle, and then it was a matter of deciding how we could film it and getting started. By Wednesday it was in the can. It was something we dreamed up on the booze, but the commercial won second prize at the Cannes festival and the cameraman has never looked back – that was Roger Donaldson.

We spent a lot of time together when Barry lived at Te Teko. We went hunting and fishing, he helped run safaris for clients, we kept filming, and Barry did some more ads for Land Rover.

By that stage he'd met Vanda and I was best man at their wedding. They tied the knot at the Whakatane registry office, then my wife Noelene looked after their two kids while Barry, Vanda, her father and I went up the river for a marvellous day in my jet boat. We all got very drunk on whisky and beer and that was the honeymoon.

I am very fond of the bagpipes. Barry and I used to pack them in to the bush and have a lot of tremendous laughs with them. We loved being outrageous and playing the bagpipes in the bush was one of those outrageous things. People couldn't get to grips with these two rough bloody bushmen playing the bagpipes in the middle of the night. It used to just tear them apart.

One time we were down at Matawai making a promotional film. The guy that was president of the outfit we were making the film for was also a member of the New Zealand Scottish Society, but he didn't know I played the bagpipes. The last night, when all the film was in the can, everyone got on the turps and he was in to the whisky something ferocious. We were in from Matawai in an old semi-derelict house and twenty-five kilometres from nowhere. It was a cold winter night, so we had an open fire and we were all sitting around the table drinking booze when this guy says, "I can hear the pipes."

"Tell you what, mate, I think you've had too much to drink," says Barry.

"No, no, I can definitely hear them."

There are six other people at the table and this poor prick is the only one who can hear the bagpipes.

"You can't hear the pipes, mate," says Barry. "Miles from anywhere in the middle of the bush, you must be joking. By Christ, mate, I think you'd better give up the whisky."

When I eventually walked in the door playing the pipes he was sitting under the table crying his eyes out. We pulled some unbelievable stunts.

Barry came and went and might disappear for the odd year or so, but he was one of those guys who could walk in the door and say, "Johnston, you bastard," and it was all on again. We had a very close friendship, one of those rare ones. A lot of people said they were friends of Barry Crump but they didn't even know him. Very few people really knew Barry. Very few knew the depth of the man.

The tragedy of five boys drowning at one of our bush camps in August 1969 was something terrible we had to survive together and it brought us closer. With many people it would have torn them apart. We were both charged with manslaughter, and it was a very long, desperate six months for us until the charges were dropped before the case went to trial.

It's been a nightmare I've had to live with ever since. People may have thought Barry was callous. He wasn't at all, but that was his way of handling it. It was the most terrible trauma for us. He changed, he withdrew an awful lot into himself for some time. It wasn't that he was avoiding reality, it was because the tragedy was so hard for him to handle. He withdrew into his shell and we probably drank too much, but that's when you know what a friend's all about.

I could always draw on Crumpy's quietly spoken advice or wisdom in times of stress or trauma. He would listen closely and then say, "You're okay, matey, you and I know that. You'll be stronger 'cause it happened. Don't let them get you down." We shared a depth of understanding built by various experiences and adventures. Crumpy loved my statement, "Life is the sum total of your experiences." Without them you have no way of really knowing life in its fullness.

I spent time with Crumpy when he lived down south with Robyn, but I didn't get to know Maggie until they shifted to Welcome Bay. I live by the sea looking out to White Island, with a boat ramp on the corner of my property, and Crumpy and I had some lovely days fishing together. "Right," said Crumpy, "we're going to spend a fair bit of time doing just that."

Not long before he died we were sitting out there in the boat. "Well, George," said Barry, "it's back to the old haunts and the things I love most. I've been through all the bullshit, don't need that any more. This is my life. Anyone else would need to live to be 200 years old to do what you and I have done."

And he was right. We packed a hell of a lot of life into a short time.

I'd never been so bone-weary or footsore or happy as when I sat by the fire that evening and told and retold a bored Stan, an exasperated Pat, and an unconscious Trevor, how I'd shot that old hind in the creek-head. They didn't know how important that deer was to me.

— *A Good Keen Man*

JON ZEALANDO
(MAGICIAN)

It's Barry's voice that stays with me, that deep, rich voice of his. The first time I heard it must have been soon after A Good Keen Man was published. I was asleep one Sunday morning after a late show and my father rushed in, woke me and insisted I get out of bed and listen to Barry Crump reading from his book on the radio.

It was such a wonderful voice and I thought I'd really like to meet the man. Then during the late 1960s, when *Town and Around* was one of the most popular shows on television, I'd been brought in for a skit the producer had dreamed up. I was going to be a pirate burying treasure on an island in the Hauraki Gulf. Barry Crump was supposed to come along and, abracadabra, I would turn him into a rabbit. The rabbit would then appear on Keith Bracey's desk (he was the frontman on the show) and speak in Crumpy's gravelly voice, asking when the hell he was going to be let out of there. The whole joke turned on the unexpectedness of hearing the good keen man's voice coming out of one of my little white rabbits. Well, this was my first experience of Crump's reliability, or lack of it. He never showed, and the skit went ahead with a ring-in and fell somewhat flat.

A few years later I was at a party at his brother Colin's place and I was quite excited to meet Barry. I'd read some of his books by then. We'd had a few drinks and I did the smoking thumb trick. That appealed to him. I do a lot of bird whistling noises and he was very curious. I use an old invention, a device called a Swiss Warble which I've kept to myself over the years.

Barry invited me to visit him any time, and eventually I did drive down to his place in Waihi. When my wife Janet and I arrived, Barry's wife Vanda didn't know who we were. Barry was in bed with a bad back, so I said not to bother him, but he came to the door.

"Hang on, hang on," he said, and made us welcome.

"How'd you get your bad back?" I asked him.

"Can't tell you that story," was all he'd say for a while. Eventually it came out. He'd hurt his back mowing the lawns.

They lived in an old settler homestead looking down a valley with a spacious front lawn. "Do you know anything about playing croquet?" he asked me. All I knew was that it was a game for old ladies, hardly Barry Crump's style, I thought. "It's quite a good game," he said, so the first thing he did was teach me how to play croquet.

Barry had a leaning towards mystical things and seemed a bit influenced by a local healer in Waihi who preached the psychic surgery stuff people were falling for hook, line and sinker at the time. Barry had made a cardboard pyramid: you were supposed to put a blunt razor blade underneath and it would sharpen overnight. He would be standing by the fireplace and suddenly he'd say to me, "I think I'm doing a telepathy thing with old (whoever it was) down the road now. I think he might be standing by his fireplace. We'll ring him up." I don't know if Barry really believed it. He could have been having me on, but he was searching.

I was sympathetic, at least, to Barry's interest, but I cast some doubt on this psychic stuff. He was very interested to find out what I knew about the trick methods of doing such things, and what I could tell him I did. I also gave him a Swiss Warble and got him whistling and later he wrote me a note saying he was driving his wife crazy with it.

Barry suggested to the local Waihi A & P Association that they book me and The Great Benyon for a two-man show at the Waihi Town Hall. That was a wonderful trip for me, just listening to Barry and Benyon swapping stories. I sat and absorbed it all but I wish now I'd had a tape recorder.

Barry had organised for me to promote the two shows the day before by doing a straitjacket escape from one of those cranes used for lifting telegraph poles, a crane of suspect quality, I thought. But anyway, there I was, suspended head down from a chain above the main street of Waihi, proving my worth. The matinee was quite well patronised because of the children, but the evening show was a bit of a flop because of two other functions happening the same night. So Barry's attempt at being the entrepreneur didn't quite come off. I am very proud that this led to a mention in his autobiography.

I remember going to see him while he was living in a van at Judges Bay, Parnell. Barry was interested in television and had been writing down ideas for skits in a little book. We chatted and I asked him how he liked boating.

There he was, living right beside the harbour, and he wasn't all that sure about being off dry land. I had an aluminium runabout and I suggested I take him out fishing to see if he liked it.

There was a harbour pilots' strike on at the time and Barry and I got all excited working up an idea for a skit in which we called ourselves the 'pirate pilots'. We'd claim we were going out in the boat to take over the pilots' jobs. I had a captain's hat – a souvenir from a cruise ship – and a funny American certificate which I would claim was my captain's qualification. It was a bit complicated, but very much to do with current affairs. There had been a dispute with a ferry operator called Dromgoole, who had a head-on collision with the Seaman's Union over manning levels on the Waiheke hydrofoil, and one of us was going to claim to be the extra seaman who never got the job the union was fighting for. While waiting for the job, he was supposed to have been circumnavigating Puketutu, an island the size of a pocket handkerchief near the sewage ponds in Manukau Harbour.

I came home and nodded off and about 11 pm woke with a start. I knew Crump had rung television and they said they'd turn up the next day to film us, and I panicked. At 1 am I was down in the basement putting the name 'SS Stirrer' on the back of the boat with black sticky tape and 'Pilots' on the sail.

I had to get the boat up on top of the Volkswagen van, and the next day I tore down there with my hat and a few things for Barry to wear and set up at Judges Bay. There were people standing watching and peering out from behind curtains. My image was quite straight as a magician and I was going to have to do this with my best Kiwi accent, trying to be a mate of Barry Crump's. We waited and waited, and television didn't turn up, so Barry said he'd go up the road to a lady friend's and telephone.

Which left me on my own feeling a bit foolish, and after a while it occurred to me that maybe this was a gag. Eventually he did come back, saying television couldn't film until the next day, but by this time I chickened out, which was a sad mistake. I'd have loved to have been his Scotty in later years.

Barry gave me a miner's lamp to look after when he went on his trip to England and drove home through India on a motorbike. I can't remember why he gave it to me – something to do with a trick I used in magic shows – but he said, "Here, take this, I'll get it back from you later." That was the way he did things.

He and Robyn came and parked their van for about a week on our back lawn under the Mangere Mountain. I got the impression that he had gone overseas looking for some truths. I queried him about telepathy and psychic things and he still half-believed in the supernatural. But in the end, he said, the more involved he got the less he felt it led anywhere, that it didn't lead to happiness and wasn't fulfilling, which was quite an interesting observation.

He told me that since the tragedy when five kids were drowned at one of his bush camps he had stopped performing for people, that his attitude was more professional. Before then he was enjoying the euphoria of being famous and he'd been one of those guys you'd buy a few drinks and he'd tell yarns and show off. He told me he'd stopped being "a bit of a galah", those were his words.

That week when they stayed at our place I took him to a Variety Artists Club tournament at the Papatoetoe Golf Club, and he met a lawyer guy, Noel Agnew, who used to be with a band, called Uncle Albert's Orgasmic Orchestra, which had been popular for a while. They got each other going with yarns and all of a sudden Barry, who'd had a few drinks, came out with "Eskimo Nell", which he was claiming had been written by the poet Robbie Burns. He knew all fifty or so verses of absolute obscenity. It was hilarious and just wonderful to be there. If only I'd taped that, his voice was just lovely.

During those couple of weeks I also took him out to a country and western night with Rusty Greaves. Rusty was a Kiwi country and western singer with fourteen kids, a builder who was never short of a naughty yarn for smoko. There was a bit of a hoe-down, and at some stage when we were out on the floor Barry grabbed me. I don't want to make a big thing about it, but I'm sure I'm one of the few men Barry Crump has hugged and kissed.

For me Barry Crump was very special, and I was always a great admirer of his talent. I was a poor reader and his books were among the few that I could get into easily. We shared secrets about our real-life desires. For me, what brought us together was the chance to experience some of the adventures that I always wanted to. He was like an older brother to me. For him, it was to satisfy his curiosity about the truths of magic and psychic things.

I was known for doing all sorts of weird things like getting darts fired in my back, laying on beds of nails and performing underwater escapes like Houdini. But that wasn't exactly the true me. Barry had the macho image of roughing it, shooting, fishing and telling yarns, but I don't know that he was that macho. I think he was quite a gentle, sensitive person in many ways.

BRYCE PETERSON
(Musician and fellow Baha'i)

It was back in the early sixties when I first met Brother Barry along with James K. Baxter and a few of his mates from *Town and Around*. We used to meet in the Victoria Pub in Victoria Street, Auckland.

Jimmy wasn't so well known as a poet to the public but he was always an oddball type of bloke, with a long scraggy beard and a fairly good thirst, who would belie his oddness with some amazing phraseology and verse.

Barry at that time was much more in the public eye. I can't really explain why he befriended me but I felt then as I do now, that it was a privilege to be included in his company and have him visit my home regularly.

At that time I was married to Dorothy and my two sons, Rickey and Carey, always loved having Barry around. There was nothing superficial about him. What you saw on television was the same guy who swapped experiences and shared songs in our kitchen on many a night. His wife Vanda and sons Lyall and Alan became part of our family, and both our sons are still very close.

Let me also say here that there were times I wished I hadn't known him . . . like the time Barry and I climbed this mountain in the Ureweras lugging a couple of heavy saddles in search of a pair of horses he'd let out to graze several months earlier. At the top of the mountain we sat down, rolled a couple of smokes and got into this very deep conversation about God.

It wasn't an argument or anything, but at that time Barry needed some convincing as to the existence of God. Having spent three years at Wesley College I was a firm believer but, considering my past form as a junkie, safe-cracker, children's song writer and fairly slack family man, I felt most inadequate to introduce Brother Barry to the teachings of Jesus. The odd thing was, as I later found out, the mountain we were on was named by the Tuhoe as Tu Haka, or the Challenge, and when I think about it now, sitting up there among the clouds, we must have been sitting on God's front porch!

Having both said our piece we agreed to go in peace and set about saddling up our horses for the descent. I tell you, riding that horse down the greasy clay slopes of Tu Haka and onto the river flats was the most hair-raising adventure I've ever experienced. Earlier on I'd sort of implied to Barry that I'd done a bit of horse riding in my time, which in truth was on the back of an old draught horse on my uncle's farm at Ngatea when I was nine, and a bit of a stunt on a horse I rode when I played hookey from Mount Albert Grammar when I was twelve. Barry had already figured this out, and this was his way of letting me know.

As soon as that horse hit the shingle on the riverbed he became Pegasus possessed. Thank Hollywood for Roy Rogers and the Lone Ranger! I just stood in the stirrups, held the reins with one hand and committed myself to the Holy Spirit. About two miles along the track I looked around and there was Barry with this massive grin twenty yards behind me as I finally pulled up.

"Didn't know you could ride like that, Brother Bryce!" he said with a tongue-in-cheek casualness.

"Nor did I, Brother Barry!" I wheezed.

"Tomorrow we'll take them for a real workout, Brother Bryce."

"Pig's bloody clankers we will, Brother Barry!" and we both left it at that.

Not long after that I teamed up with Jackson Paul Bennett and we formed a duo called Spotted Dog touring the schools, so our paths crossed in spasms until, a few years later, Brother Barry arrived at my door and informed me that I wouldn't be seeing him for a while as he was heading off in search of God. Away he went with Vanda and the boys in tow.

Months went by until one day after he'd come back from India (*pictured left*), he arrived unannounced, a mere bag of bones but with a gleam in his eyes I hadn't seen before, and proclaimed, "I've found it!"

"What?" I asked cautiously.

"God – I've found God!" he beamed. "Baha'ullah!"

"Ba – what?" I quizzed suspiciously.

I shouldn't have asked that question. I'd just pulled the pin out of a flood gate and what an earful I got. Three hours of it!

It seemed that he'd arrived back in New Zealand several days earlier after spending several months in the hills of Kashmir with some very spiritual people. But he still hadn't quite attained fulfilment until he'd arrived back here and visited an old girlfriend called Lenna, who gave him a book to read called *The Hidden Words of Baha'ullah*. The Baha'i prophet Baha'ullah had amassed thousands of followers since his appearance in the 1850s.

At the time I was working on an old tug boat called the *Miro*, towing barges up and down the coast. So Barry offered to drive me down to the western viaduct as we were due to sail around seven that evening. By now I had conjured up pictures of Barry in long, flowing sheets, shaven head and armed with a tambourine in one hand and a begging bowl in the other. It wasn't a pretty vision, so I discreetly let him know that I had some reservations about the authenticity of his new faith.

He was a cunning bastard, that Barry.

"Do you think so, matey?" he said with a pseudo humbleness. "Look, do us a favour. I might be making an idiot of myself. Read this and when you find the flaw, let me know will you?"

With that he handed me a very thin little book titled *The Baha'i Writings on Music*.

He was going straight for the jugular, knowing I loved music.

"Sure, mate, I'll read it – couldn't be fairer than that," I said and gratefully slid out of the van.

I drew first watch as we headed up the harbour on an overnighter to Mangonui, north of Whangarei. It was a beautiful night with a full moon and the old *Miro* knew the journey better than me and virtually steered herself, so I reached around to my hip pocket in search of my baccy when out came the book.

Well, I did promise, so I read it – I couldn't find any flaws and even found myself agreeing with everything . . . so I read it again – and again.

By this time it was Bluey's turn on the wheel, so I went below to put him on the shake.

"Hey, Blue – ever heard of a bloke named Baha'ullah?"

"Ba – who?"

"Baha'ullah! He's the return of Christ!"

"Oh yeah? How much an ounce are you paying for that stuff you're smoking?" was his parting shot as he climbed on deck and headed for the wheelhouse.

Me – I was blown away. I grabbed all my *Playboys* and the hypodermic I kept just in case, and threw them all over the side.

That was a number of years ago. I've given up trying to find the flaw in the Baha'i message and continue trying to live the Baha'i life, but it ain't easy. The devil in me pushes me off the tracks occasionally, but at least I've seen the light. They say that life is a jungle and in my jungle Brother Barry will always be the tallest tree. Stand proud. I owe you one! Allah'u'abha. Baha'ullah says, "In the garden of thine heart plant nought but the rose of love." Barry planted mine.

The Baha'i writings are voluminous, and I soaked them up, reading day and night. I had to buy candles because I was flattening the battery in the van. The weeks went by. I got to know the rose gardeners and always had a rose or two in the van. The police on patrol at night would drop by for a brew of tea and a yarn. As soon as they were gone I'd get back into reading. I was finding answers to questions I'd been asking all my life.

— *The Life and Times of a Good Keen Man*

TED AND CHRIS CLARK
(Golfing Companions)

Ted: When Barry first started at Radio Pacific in 1981 he was a bit nervous about being a talkback host. He'd done television but that was back in the sixties and radio was totally new for him. So he asked me if I could ring him first thing to break the ice and get him going in the morning. That was okay but I would have to be someone else, I said. I'm an American, so we settled on me being Yukon Bill, an adventurer calling in from the Yukon via satellite rigged up on his truck, and when we were on air we played on that, with my dogs getting messed up in the satellite and things like that.

For Barry's first ten or twelve shows, I set the alarm clock for 5 am, rang in and cracked a few jokes to get things started, and we had a hell of a laugh. Even old Wally, Barry's father, used to call in with a few jokes. After that, Barry was warmed up and I didn't bother dragging myself out of bed.

Chris: And after they'd finished the show, it was still some ungodly hour of the morning and we'd join Barry and Robyn for a game of golf, either at Waitakere or Barry's brother Colin's nine-hole course. We were very close in those days, the four of us.

Ted: I think it was because we were two couples, and it seemed to work. I probably saw the most of Barry during the time he and Robyn were together. We all got on very well and Chris and I were very fond of Robyn. Barry and I sort of liked each other but he was a very elusive person. I'd already decided Barry didn't have much choice about being my friend. When

I had the opportunity to see him I'd hunt him out because he had this great sense of humour that I loved and he was such a wonderful story teller. I wanted to be around him.

I'd met Barry in 1962, although I didn't see him very much at that time. Chris got to know Barry a bit later, in about 1980, when she and I got together.

In the early seventies, before Barry met Robyn, he had parked his Combi van at Judges Bay in Parnell and was living there.

"Barry," I said, "how do you get away with this?"

And that night the cops came by and stopped.

"Everything all right, Barry?" they asked.

"Yeah, thanks very much," he said, and off they went.

I went to see him at Whitianga at one stage, where he was staying on a farm. He'd turned what might have been a small sharemilker's barn into a little house with a garden. I took some wine with me and to cool it down I put it in the river, which was only about twenty metres from the house. The water was freezing. We were working away, cutting trees down for the farmer not far from the river.

"You ever go swimming in that river?" I said to Barry, knowing how bloody cold the water was.

"Oh yeah," said Barry, "all the time. We dive off, it's deep right here, Ted."

"Okay, Barry, how about a swim? We'll both just dive in, okay? We'll do it at the same time."

So I dived in and I was out the second I hit the water. I was standing when Barry came up in the middle of the river, gasping. I didn't think he was going to get back to the bank, and I thought I was going to have to go in and pull him out.

For a while, Barry tried to give me the position of holder of the "Eskimo Nell" story – although I might not have been the only one he'd tried that on. According to Barry he was the keeper of "Eskimo Nell" in New Zealand and he wanted to pass the job on. The thing about "Eskimo Nell" is that you're not allowed to write it down, you can't tape-record it and every now and again another verse comes along. Now I never could remember it all but I remember him trying hard with me.

But someone did tape Barry reciting all fifty-two verses, and Barry's brilliant. You had to have more or less only men in the bar because it got a little bit close to the mark, quite filthy really, and Barry would bring down the house.

Barry could tell a story in a way which kept you spellbound. Everyone would roll around on the floor laughing and he couldn't help himself, he could make you laugh and bring things to life.

Chris: When we were staying with Barry and Robyn in Opotiki their shithouse was a tin shed right in the middle of the paddock a hundred metres away. Ted was in there one morning having his constitutional when

Barry decided it was time to give him a fright and started firing at him from the kitchen with a .22.

Ted: God, do I remember it. Bang! "Don't stand up, Ted." Bang! bang! It put me back about two days.

Chris: For a while, when Barry and Robyn were whizzing around in their Dormobile van, we gave them the key to our house at Torbay and they'd let themselves in for a shower or to do their washing. Once, quite early on, when I didn't know Barry very well, I came home and found him looking through my kitchen cupboards.

"Can I help you, Barry?" I said. "Are you looking for something?"

"Yeah, have you got any Ajax?"

I was amazed. The good keen man was going to do some cleaning. I found it for him and asked him what he wanted it for.

"Oh, I want to clean my teeth," said Barry. He had some false teeth which got him into trouble much later when he was staying with us again.

Ted: He swallowed his plate eating a meat pie. He actually swallowed his false teeth. He would have been hungry, knowing Barry. If he ate a pie, believe me, he took half of it in a bite. Did we ever hear the end of that story?

Chris: Oh yes, he got the plate back eventually.

Ted: He stayed a lot with us over the years, at Chris's home in Torbay, our home in Paihia, our home in Whangaparaoa. He would just all of a sudden up and go. He'd be here for three or four days and then he'd be gone. But I understood him perfectly. I stayed with him at his place in Newmarket and at his whare up in Henderson, and we both stayed several times with them at their place in Opotiki. The people that owned the farm in Opotiki used to take over the house for holidays, so we stayed with Robyn and Barry both in the house and in the A-frame whare he built for himself on the property.

One time we went down to see them at Opotiki and they were away in Wellington. We stayed there on our own for about three days before they turned up, and we were enjoying the incredible solitude. Then we settled down with four of us in this little A-frame for three or four days. It was very rough but that was Barry and Robyn, they lived a bit rough. It took us away from the city and we didn't mind. It was cool, as long as Chris could do the cooking.

Barry never was very commercial. Colin and I used to try to get him to put his name to some hunting knives in the early days but he never would. He just wasn't very interested in money until he got older. The Toyota deal suited him, it didn't take anything away from him.

Chris: I kept saying to him, "There's all this money you're starting to get from Toyota, you've got to start thinking about when you get old and you're not going to have anywhere to put your hat down. Why don't you ask the owners [at Opotiki] if they'll sell it to you if you like it here?" I think that's why they bought it.

Ted: Coming up that road was the most amazing thing. I had bought a four-wheel-drive because it was the only way I could get over to see him. The first time we went up we met a lot of the neighbours. The second time we came up the road it was almost like the telegraph had sent a message – all the neighbours were at the gate to see who was coming. They'd wave, and then within no more than an hour at least four groups arrived at Barry's and stayed as long as they were allowed, until Barry gave them the message after three or four hours or when the booze was gone.

I always said to Barry, "Barry, I love your books but, you know, I'm supposed to be your friend, you should be giving them to me and if you're going to do that you might as well send me the first copy of the first edition." And that's why I've got all these books, Barry's first copies, first editions, signed.

Barry based different characters in his books on people we knew, like George Johnston. But mainly he took off his brother Bill. I believe that in all Barry's books there was a character he based on Bill to a degree, because Bill is the true original, straight as a die. But what a character! He could do anything, he could fix any truck, any boat, anything. Bill is just enormous in his abilities and I guess everyone kind of envied him that, Barry particularly. Any time he had any trouble, Bill could fix it.

They called each other Brother and after a while I became part of the Brotherhood. We all used to drink together, out at the Kowhai Social Club, which was actually a shed at Bill and Colin's factory in Henderson which we took over for our drinking. Brother Colin, Brother Barry, Brother Bill, Brother Les, Brother Ted and the others.

The Thursday before Barry died we suddenly decided to ring him. We hadn't seen him since he and Maggie shifted north and we'd changed address, so I wanted to let them know where we were and that there was always a bed with us. I knew that if Barry was in the area he would eventually turn up. He said, "I'll put it in my black book. Not my little black book – it's not so little any more, it's quite big."

The last thing he said to us was, "I'm in my spa pool right now and I can see all Tauranga."

It was the strangest thing, though. "Gosh he sounds good," I said to Chris after the phonecall. He sounded better than I'd ever heard him. He was serene, his voice was relaxed and calm, there wasn't any hype.

And that's the last time we spoke to him. I know now that Barry also rang people that day that he hadn't made contact with for a while. I'm quite sure, knowing the sort of person Barry was, that he must have known he was dying. I think he chose his own way of going. He didn't want to be in the hospital with people sending cards, I'm sure of that.

He was his own man. That's why he was larger than life, not because of his writing so much (he would have been that way if he had never written a book) but because he was a true man.

By this time the goats were making some impression on the weeds on his place. In fact, he was getting short of feed for them and they were getting harder to keep in. He had to start buying goat pellets for them, a very costly thing to do. . . . Everywhere Maisie went she was knee-deep in goats, all clamouring for a feed of goat nuts. She believed it was because they loved her, but they'd have cheerfully trodden her to death in the mud to get at a pocketful of goat nuts.

~ *Forty Yarns and A Song*

ALEX KING
(THE HOLDER OF THE NUGGET OF THE TATTOOED LEG)

We first met Barry during our annual holidays spent in the Moke Valley in the South Island. The Moke Valley and the stream of crystal clear waters had been worked for gold in earlier days and still returned good rewards for recreational miners. We were heading to a place called Moonlight Lodge to arrange a party for New Year's Eve when I saw a couple with a gold pan.

I pulled up and asked, "How's it going?"

A chap replied, "Not too good, matey."

I told him where he may find a better place to pan for gold. As I drove away I found his face familiar and later talking to others I realised that he was probably the writer, Barry Crump. On my way back down river, I checked up on the couple again. When the bloke saw me he came over smartly to show the gold he had already panned. I was taken by the sound of his voice – it was like four yards of rough gravel sliding off the steel deck of a truck. I invited him to the party that we were arranging the following night.

Little did I know that that casual meeting was the beginning of a twenty-year friendship which was as close as two men and a family could have. The letters, the phone calls, the visits – he was always there. It is a well-known fact that as a writer he never wrote any sex or foul language into any of his books. I have many beautiful letters from Barry and there is not a bad line in them. I never heard him bad mouth anyone and in the same twenty years I never heard him once take the Lord's name in vain.

Was he a saint? In some ways, yes, and in other ways, a great big no. But back to the party night. Lin Herron, runholder of Ben Lomond Station and I arrived at the site early and from our spot, looking down to the terraces from about 200 feet above, we could see two people travelling on a Honda road bike, heading our way. As they got closer I wondered how on earth they would ever manage the river crossing. The river was about sixty feet across on the angle and an average of about twenty inches deep and was filled with smooth, water-worn boulders and flat, slippery stones. We waited in anticipation as Barry and Robyn approached the river. We expected them to get a dunking. But standing on the footrests with Robyn clinging to his back, Crumpy weaved his way round every obstacle and up the track to where we sat, grinning. He killed the motor, thumbed his hat back and said, "You two bastards were hoping we'd fall off."

A crowd of about sixty partied that night with piped music, a dance floor and a bar which Barry took an interest in. When it was time to prepare the meal, Barry and I took over the massive range fired by a diesel gun burner. It was a hot summer night and with the added heat of the huge range we had all the windows open. The moths came through the open window and nose-dived onto the sixty steaks we were barbecuing on the range top. Beer in one hand and fish slice in the other, we delighted in smacking down a moth or two on top of a steak. No-one went without that night. The party flowed and so did the two cooks' friendship.

The days that followed were great. Panning for gold in Moke Creek, teaching Robyn to drive a 1942 American Jeep along the river flats. We would spend nights back at our caravan where Lorna, my wife, would cook up a big meal. Barry admitted it was a nice change from rabbits, possums and goats. By this time Lin Herron had let Barry and Robyn into the huts up at Seffers (pictured overleaf) and they were a bit better set up than in the back of the Model A that they had been living in. Food was a major item for Barry and Robyn. In the heat of summer with no fridge it was a case of eat it when it was available. We never took food back out at the end of a day's visit. The unwritten rule was leave it for your mates. Barry worked likewise, what he had was yours if you wanted it and it extended to others.

I remember once when he and I were working the Moke with the riffle box, Barry got a good size nugget – about the size of a man's thumbnail. It was the best Barry had caught to date. Back at the hut I took a lead pencil rubbing of it on a piece of newspaper to show Lorna. Barry, in his usual style, said, "Not that way, Alex." At that he put his precious nugget in a small screwtop jar and said, "Take it out and show Lorna the real thing. You're coming back tomorrow. Bring it back then."

The next day when I returned I found that there was no Robyn or Barry at the huts. They had gone to Queenstown for supplies and we had missed them on the road. I hid the jar with the nugget in it behind the top wall plate against the roof inside the hut. We went back to working the creek but after a while I thought what an obvious, stupid place to hide the thing. What if someone found it? Barry would never believe a cock-and-bull story like that. He'd think that I'd been trying to hang onto it.

We drove back up to the house. I've heard remarks like "my racing heart" and I tell you my little built-in pump on the left-hand side was overworking as my hand reached to retrieve the nugget. When it came time to hand it back to Barry, he was wearing the biggest grin I've ever seen him wear as I told him the story of my concern at the nugget being stolen.

"Oh, come on, Alex, I would have believed you anyway. There's only one part I want." With that he took the nugget out of the jar, and followed up with, "I want the jar. I've grown fond of it. The nugget is for you."

Talking of gold, listen to this gem of a story. Barry and Robyn had hit town for a couple of days and one evening over a meal in the caravan we talked about the price of gold, which had rocketed to $800 a troy ounce. Lorna asked Barry if she could buy an ounce of gold off him to see what would happen in the future to gold prices. Barry replied that she could have an ounce of gold. I insisted that we did pay and Barry replied that I could pick it up from the Moke next day. He told me where he hid his gold and the next evening we weighed out an ounce of nuggety Moke gold.

Lorna had her purse ready to pay, I was thinking wildly that he may say we could have it for about $700 – $650 would have been even better.

With a twisted grin he said, "How about $350 Lorna?" The same voice then boomed out, "And I'll tell you what, Lorna, I'll give you $50 now for a cup of coffee." Thinking of this has forced me to check today's gold price. Thanks Barry, at $550 Lorna is still on the right side of the ledger.

Years later when Barry was staying with us down in Gore on one of his many visits, I brought the nugget out to show him again. He said, "Hell, have you still got that thing? Good job I gave it to you for safekeeping. I would have lost it years ago."

Barry and my two boys got along first class. Scott was at high school and Matty at intermediate when we all met up. The boys sometimes camped up at Seffers when Barry and Robyn were setting a few traps for possums. The two boys accompanied them and Barry was forever handing out tips on how to best set traps. At this stage of his life, he was sick of killing and would always apologise to a possum in a trap for what he was about to do with the hammer he was carrying. Just a few lines like, "Please forgive me little possum, but the fact is I need your coat and where you're going you won't need it." Once he took so long apologising after he'd tapped one on the head that when he opened the jaws of the trap the possum jumped onto the tree alongside and raced to the top of it. The cursing and swearing that followed echoed around the valley walls and I was quite surprised it didn't start a shingle slide.

A mate of ours has had gold fever for years. He was always turning up with new and revolutionary gold recovery gear. Pumps and diggers, suction dredges and detectors, new types of riffles, and once, to his great embarrassment, a gold divining rod he'd sent away for. All this equipment was employed in the pursuit of Fred's burning ambition, to find a big nugget. Every weekend and holiday for years he burrowed and scavenged in the creeks and river banks in search of his big nugget. He found quite a bit of gold, but nothing bigger than the head of a four-inch nail. We used to tease him about it.

– *Forty Yarns and a Song*

Our daughter Stephanie had a brain tumour and Barry showed such concern during her illness. When she recovered she named her new horse after Barry's character, Mrs Windyflax.

There was a time I thought I'd offended him. He was staying in Queenstown for the night and we were to do a few things the next day. At three o'clock in the morning I heard his ute start up and he was gone. What had I done, I wondered, trying to think back over what I had said. I did find an answer in the months to follow. It was just that Barry Crump had shot through, and to those who knew Barry, it was always on. He would get this sudden urge to hit the track.

Years later, he rang and asked me to be best man at his marriage to Maggie. I asked when the big day would be and he replied that he'd ring me closer to the time. I hung up and told Lorna about it. "He's going to ring me when it comes a bit closer but, come morning, I'll be the only one who remembers this phone call."

I never did get that phone call, so was not at his wedding, but he did have his best mate as his best man. Barry spent a lot of time telling the Registrar of the Wanaka Court that a man always has his best mate as his best man and Matey Potato there was his best mate.

Matey Potato is a beautiful little black and white Border Collie dog who sat faithfully alongside his master when he was married. What a laugh I had – upstaged by a dog.

The last call I had from Barry was about a week before he died. He wanted us both to come up to Tauranga to see their new property which he had just finished fencing. We did make it to say goodbye to Barry. Maybe to some people he couldn't put a foot right, but in our company he never put a foot wrong. I believe he was one of the earth's better people and that we were privileged to know him the way we did.

In the last couple of years our family has been beset by serious illnesses. During this time Barry supported us, keeping in touch by mail and phone from wherever he was. When your batteries get low, you need a recharge and that's what Barry was good at. He was the most sincere, understanding and thoughtful mate a person could have. This was the Barry Crump I knew and loved.

After he died I went to Tauranga to say my last goodbyes to him. Maggie took me aside and said Barry had left something for me. She gave me a little brown bag with a gold nugget inside. It was The Nugget of the Tattooed Leg that he had written to me about over the years. (See From the Letterbox.)

We bought an old wheel-tractor with a front-end loader on it and had a big steel box made, with three layers of expandite on carpet for riffles. We'd set it up and dam the creek till we had the right amount of water running through it. I'd drop the buckets of gravel into the box and Robyn would keep the big stones moving with a garden hoe and watch for nuggets . . .

That summer we cut half an acre of hay with an old scythe and stacked it in one of the huts for winter feed for our horses. We trapped skins again through the winter and when the summer came round we resumed our mining operation. We were getting good at it. We took out a Prospecting Licence and then a Mining Licence on about a mile or our creek. We were official gold-miners.

– The Life and Times of a Good Keen Man

HELEN RASMUSSEN
(Fellow Whitebaiter)

Ian and I first met Crumpy in remote South Westland down the Ohineomaka (Black River) immediately before the 1977 whitebaiting season. We were in the process of building our hut on the kowhai-lined bank of the Black River.

Daily we would make the laborious trek in the Land Rover from the main highway down a nine-kilometre track of huge mud holes (Land Rover eating variety), creekbeds around a bluff and through bush. The first trip in we passed Barry and Robyn dragging firewood back to their camp. The next day, in a neighbourly gesture motivated by nosiness, we hooked a couple of pieces of dry totara out of the riverbed to the Land Rover and towed them up to their camp.

Following the introductions Crumpy insisted we have a brew with them. Facilities at Crumpy's hut were basic – all cooking was over a campfire outside and all water had to be carried from a creek a kilometre away. While the billy was boiling Crumpy announced he had better clean the teaspoon for the visitors. He then proceeded to gouge a build-up of condensed milk, sugar and substances unknown out with his fingernail. This concerned me slightly but not half as much as the tin mugs that the tea was presented to us in. My mug was white and well used, with numerous dribble marks down the sides and clear lip marks around the rim. I managed a couple of mouthfuls before discreetly knocking the mug over.

This began a friendship that endured until Crumpy's untimely death.

We came to know Barry as a bushman living off the land, enjoying the challenge of whitebaiting and appreciating the raw natural beauty of a remote paradise. He was a Baha'i and the sole adornment in his hut was a large picture of Baha'ullah.

Crumpy and Robyn had been in residence for three weeks before our arrival and had been living largely off the land. Their diet had consisted mainly of boiled whitebait. "After a couple of weeks boiled whitebait tends to become rather tiresome," Crumpy drawled. A possum hunter, a previous occupier of the hut, had left behind a container of flour mixed with eucalyptus for possum bait and Crumpy had made fritters out of the mixture. "It provided an interesting change," Crumpy said.

Crumpy appeared to revel in the remoteness and simple way of life. Their entire equipment and supplies for the season had been carried in by Robyn and himself in one trip. He was a dedicated whitebaiter and fished from daylight till dark. I was a frequent visitor to his stand because he was an entertaining man with a wonderful sense of humour, always ready to tell a yarn.

Crumpy had an all-purpose knife, it was a large, heavy knife with a nick out of it which was used as a bottle opener and to open cans. It was also used for skinning possums and cutting hair, and in the kitchen. The knife was cleaned with a quick wipe on the trousers. On one particular visit, Crumpy was cutting the bread with the all-purpose knife singing his version of "The First Cut Is the Deepest". His version was, "The first cut is the dirtiest, the second cut is dirty but not as dirty as the first . . ."

I soon learned to decline offers of brews when the tide was in because they were made with salt water. Crumpy thought I was fussy. I recall him catching a kahawai, rolling it in numerous layers of newspaper, wetting it thoroughly in the river and covering it in the ashes of the campfire and maintaining a good hot fire on top of the fish until it was cooked. It was absolutely beautiful.

Crumpy often expounded his dislike of material possessions. This was quite obvious from his meagre belongings, many of which had been collected from the Hokitika rubbish dump. One of my favourite and most used cookery books was a present from the Hokitika dump, along with a gold fob watch case and a storage box for Ian to use on the truck. He believed we were prone to being controlled by material belongings. This was the main reason he had gone bush. He also told us he had destroyed the manuscripts of five books because he felt the motivation for writing them had been wrong.

Robyn and Crumpy were like chalk and cheese. Robyn always seemed very contented no matter the situation, but was quite serious and there seemed to be no such thing as a joke in Robyn's world. Crumpy, on the other hand, was very laid back and was a great raconteur. Crumpy would tell a joke, then Robyn would get all logical about the punchline.

On the completion of our hut it was decided we would hold a hut-warming party. The whitebaiters were all invited, a total of eight. Crumpy and Robyn, of course, were among the guests. Robyn did not drink at all and and at that time Crumpy only drank the occasional social one. The party proceeded with Crumpy providing the entertainment both with the guitar and by telling jokes. Unfortunately, as the night wore on one guest flaked and two who were brothers became morbid. One brother had been banished down the Black by his wife and told not to return until he had caught enough whitebait to put a new roof on the house. The other brother's wife had just run off with a barman. The night concluded with the latter of the two brothers lying out the door singing, "You picked a fine time to leave me, Lucille . . ." in between throwing up, and Crumpy in the background reciting fifty-two verses of "Eskimo Nell".

Crumpy was a dedicated whitebaiter and was usually the first one to set up in the morning, generally just at daylight because whitebait start to move then. Because Crumpy didn't have a watch, time was difficult to gauge. His hut was situated a couple of kilometres from the river. The morning trek was made along a muddy, rough track in the dark with the aid of a torch made from a large jam tin with a hole cut in the side to enable you to poke a candle through. This gives a very good light unaffected by wind or rain. Crumpy's internal timing system worked fine except when it was full moon. At this time it was not uncommon to get a visit and a brew in bed at two or any other ungodly hour of the morning.

The three months we spent down the Black River were very special, in a particularly beautiful part of South Westland where one morning I counted thirty-six tuis in one kowhai tree and countless wood pigeons. It really was a paradise where we came to know and love Barry as a very special friend.

Haere ra e hoa.

Our stand was the front one, nearest the sea, but that didn't mean we were going to get any more whitebait than any of the other four stands on the river that year. We built a small jetty from the bank out into the river, with posts and timber chain-sawed out of the bush, which grew right to the edge of the water. Then we made wire-mesh screens and nets to fit between the piles of the jetty.

We'd put our nets and screens in and sit on the stand, watching for shoals of whitebait coming up the river. It was quite often possible to drive a shoal of bait into your net by plonking a stone beyond them. Another trick, I think frowned upon by rangers, was to tack a silver tin-lid onto a long pole and flash it out in the river to chase whitebait towards your nets. We were getting as much bait as any of the others, no big runs but a steady trickle with most tides.

Some whitebaiters who had a big hut half a mile up the river took out our tins of bait and brought in our supplies on their tractor. All Robyn and I had to do was fish and swim and lay round in the sun eating cold pigeon sandwiches and drinking tea. Lazy happy days, after crawling up and down the sides of the Alps all winter.

– *The Life and Times of a Good Keen Man*

GEORGE WILSON
(Gold-panner)

I FIRST MET BARRY AND HIS THEN WIFE ROBYN IN 1977. THEY WERE CAMPING OUT OF THE BACK OF AN OLD MODEL-A FORD PICK-UP WITH A LARGE CANVAS CANOPY ON IT, IN MOKE CREEK IN THE MOUNTAINS BEHIND QUEENSTOWN.

They had been playing around with gold pans and riffle boxes, finding a little gold, but had come to the inevitable conclusion that, if they were to make a living out of it, they'd need to be able to handle the material faster and easier than they could by hand. And that meant machinery. I happened to have an old Nuffield tractor with a heavy, cumbersome old industrial loader on it. We built a twelve foot by four foot riffle box out of bits of steel I had lying around and set out to make our fortunes.

We nearly lost Barry on the way. He was driving the tractor on the downhill run past Sutherland's place on Gorge Road from Arthurs Point to Queenstown. These old Nuffields have a thrust bearing in the top of the steering column that is supposed to keep everything in place. Not this one. Its various components decided to go on holiday – all at once. All of a sudden the tractor would not go where it was told.

If you can picture Barry driving an old tractor on a downhill run, on a good fast sealed surface, with brakes that hadn't worked properly for years, if ever, and in too high a gear, when the steering wheel winds out in his hands, it's not too difficult to appreciate why he decided to abandon ship as it left the road to run down a slope into a drainage ditch.

The problem was that the loader frame and the plumbing that went with it made it like climbing into a cage to get into the driver's seat. When Barry tried to bale out his leg got caught up in all this tangle of steel and hydraulic hoses, and he ended up dangling in front of one of the rear wheels as the tractor careered into the ditch. Just as Barry was about to disappear under the wheel – which would have been decidedly messy – the tractor ran smack into the only decent-sized rock in the area and stopped dead. I have no doubt that this saved his life, but the wrenching it gave his knee explains the bit of a limp that Barry had from that date forth.

While Barry was recovering from his little adventure I grafted another front end on the tractor and got it all functioning again, and we eventually got working in the Moke. We'd drop the box in the creek with the tractor, then build a dam with the loader to divert just enough water through the box, and then drop gravel into it with the loader. It was a pretty simple sort of an operation, but for Barry and Robyn it beat gold pans hands down. There was no chance of getting rich, but it paid the tucker bill, and for me it was a welcome escape from a concreting business. It got to the point where we knew the strips of 'flood gold' off various rocks and points that were replenished with each flood. And living was pretty easy and relaxed.

We ended up in partnership in a mining licence in the Moke, and some of my fondest memories are of times in the Moke and at Seffertown with Barry and Robyn, and later with Barry's brother Bill.

I recall one night, heading back to Seffertown late from Queenstown, there were three to four inches of snow on the ground and we were spotlighting possums whilst using a bottle of Black Label to keep warm. At one stage we lost the bolt for the .22, which took us a good part of the bottle to find. By the time we reached Lake Kilpatrick we had lost what good sense we may normally be credited with somewhere back up the trail.

Anyway, here was the lake, frozen over and three to four inches of snow on top of the ice. We had walked out to somewhere near the middle of the lake – which is maybe half a dozen football fields in area – when I gave voice to this chilling thought that had suddenly come to me about how sometimes when ice breaks under you, it doesn't actually leave a hole – a large slab can just sort of tip up, slide you in and close up again.

Well, you have never seen a pair of clowns sober up faster, or step lighter in all your days. As I recall, the possums on the rest of the way home were pretty safe. We alternated from deathly silence to nervous babble and back again.

The public persona that most people saw, the Crumpy of Toyota fame, and before that the larger-than-life bushman author, was a very small part of the real person. In fact, the public persona was often pretty hard work for Barry. He went through long periods of being very private and reclusive, and was at times not at all comfortable with having to play the part of the public Crumpy and the expectations that went with it.

Barry Crump the man was one of the deepest, most interesting people

I have ever known. He had experienced at first hand a greater variety of extreme, unusual, interesting activities and vocations than most people could name, let alone have experienced. He met and got to know a lot of 'out there' people.

And he learned something from every one of them.

One result of this was that he had a very broad perception and understanding. Another was that he became, in many respects, world weary, from time to time suffering from bouts of boredom and frustration. This was, as often as not, the motivation for shooting through, moving somewhere new in search of the motivating power of a new experience, a new place. It is probably fair to say that it became as much an addiction to change as anything.

Barry and Robyn were firm believers in the merits of the Baha'i faith and its capacity to solve the political and social problems of the world. The hours we have spent around the fire debating this and other topics of the soul, solving the problems of the world, will be a part of me for the rest of my days.

I remember one time camped up a river at Punakaiki on the West Coast of the South Island. Barry and Robyn went for a walk, and one of them found a tiny child's gumboot. It would have been less than three inches long. The conversation around the campfire that night turned to speculation as to whether it was the gumboot of a pixie or an elf. Barry concluded it must have belonged to one of the pungapeople, a clan of elves indigenous to New Zealand. This was the inspiration behind several poems and songs, and eventually the children's book *Mrs Windyflax and the Pungapeople*.

I know that Barry was pretty blown away by and proud of his nomination for and subsequent award of an MBE for services to literature. I believe it greatly improved his self-esteem, and his faith that what he wrote was really worth publishing. I think he even began to enjoy writing more after that.

Barry was no saint, he was as far from perfect as most of us are. But he was a good-hearted, intelligent and civilised man, if a bit rough around the edges. He was more of a thinking man than some gave him credit for. As anyone living under the public spotlight can attest, any minor misdemeanour was likely to be noticed and blown out of proportion. Still Barry managed to get through life with pretty general respect across the various spectrums of society.

In many respects he was a very lonely man. To those that he considered his mates he was a good friend, but there were very few of his friends, other than those directly involved in whatever he was currently doing, that he would ever call by telephone, and even those few, very rarely. So when, after no contact for months, he rang me three times in the space of a fortnight asking me when I was coming up, I knew things must be getting a bit strained.

Barry and his last wife Maggie with her son Anton had shot through from Wanaka, bought the fifty-six foot motor vessel *Ocean Star* and were living aboard in Picton, getting the boat sorted out for a new life in the Marlborough Sounds. But – after weeks of pouring rain and the most bleak and dismal of what Picton can offer, many thousands of dollars, and all the frustrations of confined spaces with a young boy, having to move off the boat while it was on the slip because of bylaws, and still being no closer to ready to go – he started looking for help.

By the time I got there most of the messy stuff had already been done. I did repair the new hydraulic steering gear, but other than that the only purpose I served was as crewman and moral support for the maiden voyage from Picton out and around Queen Charlotte, and around into Pelorus and down into Havelock.

By this time he and Maggie had come to the conclusion that perhaps the logistics of life aboard were not quite what they had expected. And *Ocean Star*, with her deep draught, was more restricted than they had anticipated in moving around the shallower reaches of Pelorus Sound. And, I suspect, there may have been an element of choice required, between the two women in Barry's life at that time, Maggie and *Ocean Star* – a tick on the wall for Maggie.

They ended up buying a house in Havelock and selling *Ocean Star* in Barry's typically casual fashion, losing quite a lot of money in the process. But that was Barry's way. When he was finished with something, it was gone, regardless of what losses he took in the process.

I only knew Barry for the last third of his colourful and interesting life, but in those twenty years we became good friends and spent quite a lot of time in each other's company. I suspect that he knew me better than I knew him in a lot of ways, but he had twenty years' head start to hone his perceptions. I am very much the richer for his friendship. He was a man for whom I have far greater respect than most.

"There's gold eroding out of this country all the time, and there's a hundred years worth in that creek since anyone last worked it. Some interesting things can happen to gold in a hundred years. Depends on the floods. The creek's a big rough riffle box and because of its weight the gold accumulates in certain places in the floods. If you can find those places you can pick the eyes out of it without havin' to put the whole creek through your gear."

"That makes sense. Do you know any other places where there's gold?"

"Yeah, a few."

"As much gold as Broken Creek?"

"Yeah, only most of 'em are a bit harder to get at than this."

"How did you find them?"

"Me and a few other blokes starved for years prospectin' for gold through these hills. Everyone reckoned we were mad, includin' us. We knew about these places but they weren't worth doin' until the price of gold went up in the seventies. Before that you had to find really rich ground to be worth workin', and there's not much of that left around, especially with the gear we had in them days. Most of the prospectors were older than me, and now they're too old or gone away or dead. There's none of the blokes I knew left."

– Gold and Greenstone

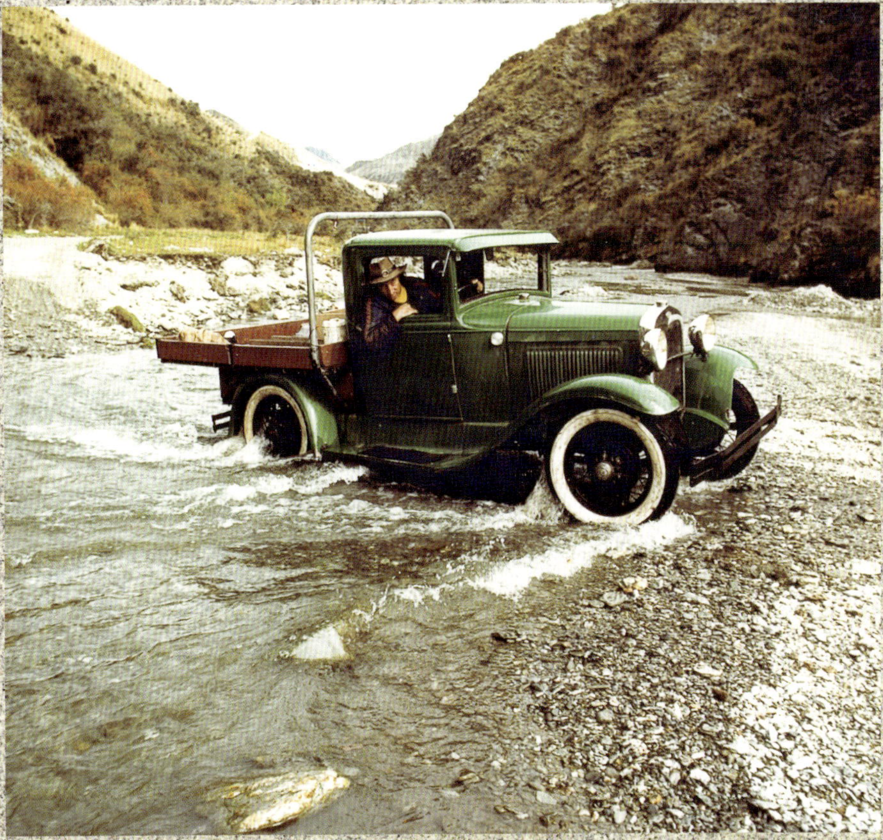

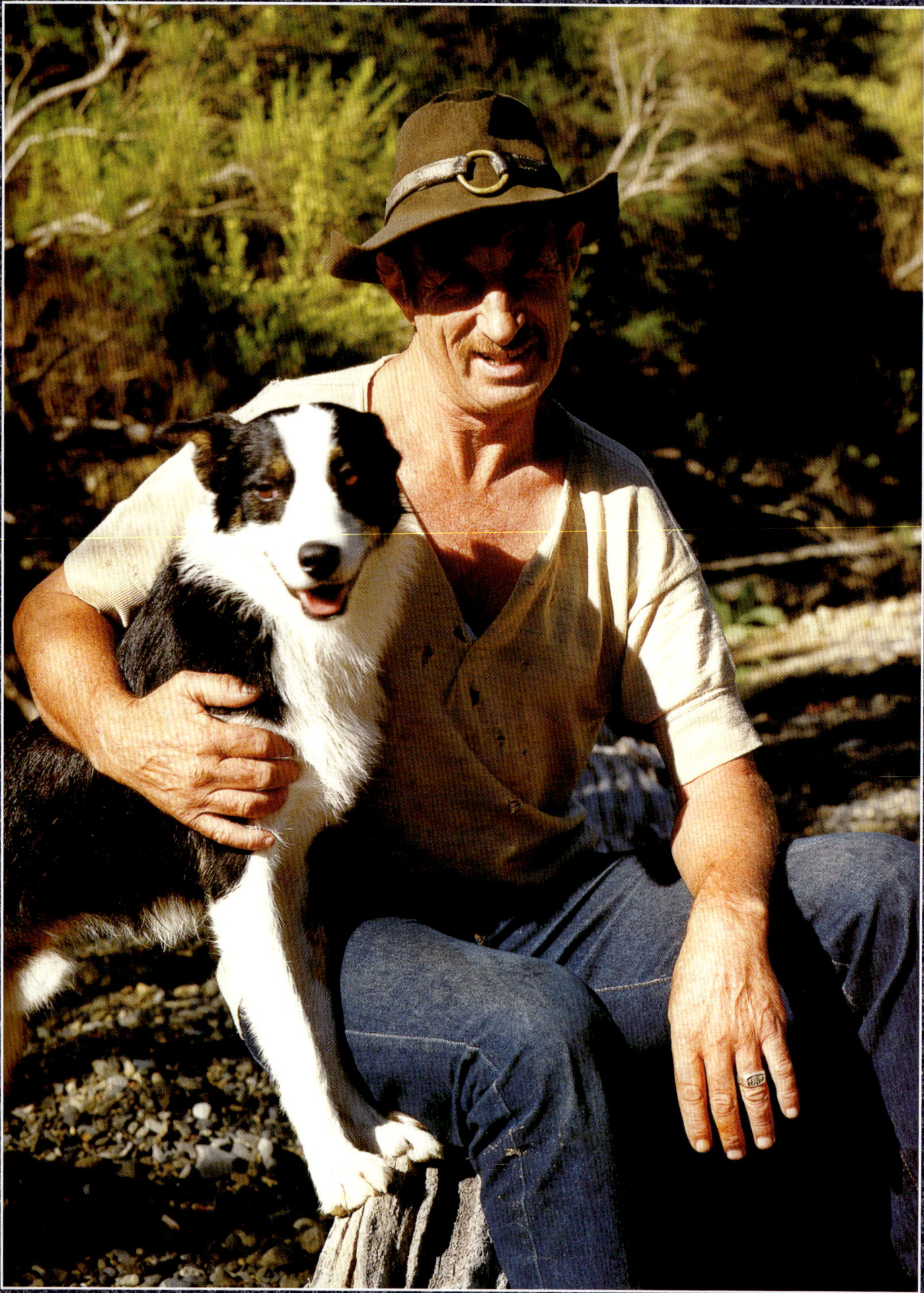

Chapter 5
Gold and Greenstone

By the time they'd paid for the gearbox, a tank of gas and a bit of other stuff, they had sixty dollars left. Before they left town Quin bought some sausages, a loaf of sliced bread and a roll of tin-foil. He wrapped six sausages in tin-foil and tied the bundle to the exhaust manifold of the ute with some wire Sally found for him on the back.

"That's our next feed," he said. "It'll take between one and two hundred ks to cook that."

Sally was impressed. This could save money if it worked.

– Gold and Greenstone

BARBARA MAGNER
(*Town and Around* Journalist)

I met Barry first in 1960 in Dunedin at a medical school party. I knew about Barry, of course, because I knew a lot of writers. I don't remember much about the party but Barry certainly stood out among student types. He was right in the middle of reciting "Eskimo Nell", which was one of his famous and appalling party pieces.

I think I heard the whole thing right through only once, but in fact I heard him perform "Eskimo Nell" many times in those days. I just used to disappear once he started because it's a very long, rambling, bawdy piece of poetry. I couldn't believe my ears when I noticed one of his television advertisements faded away with Crump starting to recite "Eskimo Nell" and I thought, the old devil. Of course, that's typical Barry getting such inflammatory stuff on prime time TV and I must admit it amused me because it was like a secret code. Anyone who knew him well has heard "Eskimo Nell" at least once.

I could see, from that first meeting, that Crump was an incredible story teller, and I was attracted to him because of that. My father told wonderful stories; it was part of our Irish tradition, the long line of story tellers we came from, and I recognised it at once in Barry. I've heard Crump tell stories and I've been in his company with other friends many, many times when we've all told jokes and stories, and they were sometimes the most exciting times of my life.

Everything that Crump said or wrote was very familiar to me because I was brought up in the country. Barry was one of the very few people I ever spoke to about how harsh and cruel I found country life. He has glorified that in a way in his writings.

This is not talked about in New Zealand, but in the early days of dairy farming, the lives of wives and children could be hard. I think it was the economist/historian W. B. Sutch who wrote that the dairy industry was made on the backs of women and children. We had this side of our lives in common.

"Yeah, I know what you're talking about," he said. He told me he had seen his sister lashed across the face with a dog chain. Growing up in the country, I was very familiar with this kind of violence, plenty of swearing and loud behaviour and cruelty to animals. It seemed the natural order of things then.

I didn't really meet him again until I joined the television current affairs programme *Town and Around* in Auckland in 1966. He wasn't a regular on staff but he'd perform as a 'ring-in', as he called himself. *Town and Around* was a fabulous time of my life and we all worked very hard. Crump used to turn up to work on the show and then disappear for awhile. When he did turn up everybody went to the pub for a few drinks and storytelling.

His television pieces, like his stories, were very popular with the public, but for Barry it was a whole new departure, thinking in pictures and being able to relate to the camera as if it were another person. I could see he was wondering if he could carry it off.

I thought he could, because anyone who could write those books had imagination. He did it his own way, of course. He simply ignored the camera and relied on the cameramen being able to follow him, and they got used to working around him.

Crump worked hard at his television pieces. I think he was very careful that the essence of the Crumpy stories came across. I don't remember his first item but I do remember the one about the truck. In this skit, he was going to take a woman to a ball and she came out in a wonderful gown with floating panels of tulle, looking very elegant. He looked rather good too, one of the few times I ever saw him in black tie and dinner suit and not his usual clobber. That was a good touch, because it had a surprise element for the audience.

So he pulled up in the truck, they got in and the motor wouldn't start. He tried and tried, with all the noise of an engine not turning over, then he got out, put the bonnet up and started fiddling. His date got out because he was taking too long, and the audience was right with the story, just waiting for the inevitable. You saw him eyeing her gown like, "This would be a go for cleaning the oil stick," and grabbing a piece of tulle off her dress. It was wonderful, and not a word said.

When Maurice Shadbolt and I were living in Titirangi, Crump and his wife Vanda turned up out of the blue in a huge new station wagon. In those days station wagons had the sort of appeal Land Cruisers do today, they were very much the 'in' thing. Maurice and I went out to greet them and we hadn't even got back to the house when we were roaring with laughter as Crump told this amazingly funny story about the new electronic windows and how he'd managed to lock the keys inside. It was typical of a Crump story, the way he saw the absurd or the memorable in the most everyday events and turned them into jokes.

Not too long after that (it was 1972 and I was pregnant) we went to Barry and Vanda's big old house in Waihi with Maurice's four children. Maurice and Crump played croquet and Vanda and I talked and looked at the house.

They offered me their bassinet. It was a bit battered-looking but I was pleased – I knew buying one was probably out of the question. Crump had all these children but somehow I didn't associate him with a bassinet.

I don't think he was entirely happy a lot of the time. He was a driven kind of person, but he gave people a lot of pleasure.

I got into doing interviews and skits for the producer of a television show called *Town and Around* and learnt not to worry about the camera.

I did some fairly hard-case interviews in those days. A friend recently reminded me of the time the head of a major English publishing-house (it might have been Collins) arrived in Auckland and because I had written books the producer asked me to interview him in the studio. They introduced us and sat us down and cued me to start.

"What's the guts of publishing caper you're into, me old mate?" I said. "Tell us a bit about that."

I don't remember how the rest of the interview went, but there had to be a laugh in it.

Television was new here then and it was all go. I still reckon that some of the best local television we've had yet was done back in the old black-and-white days. None of us knew what we were doing but we were having fun doing it, and in that respect making television material seems to me to be a bit like writing. If it's fun to do, it's fun to watch. Laboured writing usually turns out hard to read. With me it does, anyway.

– The Life and Times of a Good Keen Man

CLIFF JOSEPHS
(Former Publisher)

CRUMPY CERTAINLY SAW ME COMING. AT THE TIME WE SIGNED HIM AS AN AUTHOR I WAS SALES DIRECTOR FOR BECKETT STERLING. WE WERE BASICALLY BOOK DISTRIBUTORS, AND HAD DECIDED TO DEVELOP A publishing list. I knew that Crump had tried publishing his own titles with moderate success and he had just started his Toyota ads. He'd done a book called *Shorty* about golfing and I'd heard he still owed a printer a reasonable amount of money.

Crump and Robyn were living about thirty kilometres out of Opotiki towards the Ureweras on a farmlet running a few goats. There was no phone on at the farm, and I had to phone and leave a message for him at the pub. The message got through, we arranged to meet and I drove down from Auckland. There I was, a new boy in publishing, a new car, the latest Italian suit and Italian shoes, and I walked in to the public bar of the Opotiki Hotel and introduced myself. There was a bit of a silence.

"How are you," said Crump, and just looked at me. It wasn't that easy but we sank a few Steinies. "You'd better come home," he said.

He must have decided to have a bit of fun with me.

Crump had a four-wheel-drive and I followed him in my brand-new BMW along a narrow, winding back road until he disappeared from sight. He must have been going pretty fast because I was going flat tack to keep up with him. I came over the brow of a hill and ploughed straight into a river crossing. I buried the car's nose in. There was Crumpy, waiting for me. He hadn't bothered to tell me there was a crossing. "That was pretty good, mate," I said, coming up alongside him.

"Do you want to have a go taking her across the ford?" said Crump.

No way. I left the car on one side of the river and drove across with him. When we got to his place they were out of water. He used water to drive a Pelton-wheel to generate electricity, and the water pipe up in the hills had come loose.

"Do you want to come up and give me a hand?" said Crump. Less of a question than a statement.

We headed straight off up to the top of a cliff in the foothills overlooking his small home. Crump was wearing boots, but I still had my Italian shoes on. Once we found the problem, Barry had to secure the pipe again to get the water flowing. It was attached by a rope as the weight of the pipe was incredible.

"Here, hold this," he said, shoving the rope into my hands.

It was very heavy and after about ten minutes I couldn't hold it any longer. I said, "Stuff this," and let it go, showering Crump with water.

"You bastard!" yelled Crump, absolutely furious. "I was just waiting until you let go. I wondered how long you'd last."

I thought he was going to hit me. I took off, sprinting down the hill with Crump chasing me through the bush, but I was pretty quick for a city boy and kept ahead of him.

After he'd chased me around the bush a bit, I said, "Quits, we want to talk about business," so we sat down and had a few drinks. We'd taken up another dozen Steinlagers and a bottle of Black Label whisky. Where they lived was nothing more than a shack, a little whare with a bedroom and an open fire where they cooked in a big black pot. It was really primitive, but they liked it that way. We drank on for a while and then he said it was too late to take me back out so I might as well stay. We were a bit drunk by then so I said okay. Robyn served from the black cooking pot a surprisingly tasty meal of soup and bits. We still hadn't settled on any arrangement by that stage to publish his books. He told me I had to sleep upstairs in a loft and when I got up there it was full of mosquitoes and possum skins. I guess he was testing me out again.

Even half-sloshed I couldn't sleep and halfway through the night I tried to creep into bed with Crump and Robyn to keep warm. No show. He wasn't letting me in. In the end I managed to sleep beside him on top of the bed.

In the morning we went down to the river, stripped off and had a cold swim, which was brass monkey stuff. But at this stage I didn't really care what was happening.

Then we had a chat. "Look, you've got a problem up north," I said. I said if he let us republish his books and revamp them we'd pay his printer's bill off and do a deal.

"Where have you been all my life, mate?" Crump said, shook my hand and that was it. Deal done.

We went on to publish three new books and revamp and republish all his old ones. We had a tremendous launch for a book called *Wild Pork and Watercress* down near his place in Opotiki in a beautiful setting near a river. To get there you went on a very bumpy gravel road which had a sheer drop on one side and was only suitable for four-wheel-drive vehicles. It was all orchestrated. We'd got all the guests in and Crumpy was supposed to come in by helicopter carrying a wild boar which he'd killed, with Scotty down in the bush yelling, "Barry!" for the TV cameras and the media.

Barry was about an hour late and when he arrived he was mobbed. It wasn't really his thing but it was a lot of fun. The Maori people from the district cooked the food for us. In the end we had about fifteen dozen beer left over, and I stayed behind with a couple of helpers to clean up. There I was, with two young ladies, and I looked back towards the track and saw the Mongrel Mob arriving in their old Chevies. They pulled up in a big circle and sat there looking at us.

"We're in trouble," I thought, but I offered them some beer and that took care of things temporarily. I was wondering how we were going to get out of there, though, because no one had come back to pick us up yet. Next minute I heard the thud-thud-thud of helicopters coming through the hills like *Apocalypse Now*, and in came the cavalry – Barry's other guests, the deerstalkers, had turned up for the party, and in the end they arranged for our transport out. As we left we could see red diff oil all over the track where the Mob had bottomed their cars. It was a great party.

I stayed that night at the hotel in Opotiki, and in the morning I found, roped over the front of my BMW, the pig that Crumpy had brought in for the launch, blood and guts everywhere. I guess he won in the end.

My dealings with Crumpy were always memorable and never dull.

The boar had his haunches safely tucked into the bank on the far side of the creek and was making nearly as much noise as Flynn, who was diving back and forth in the water trying to get the pig to run so he could get in behind him. That boar really knew his business; he was waiting his chance to catch the dog unawares and get his tusks into him. I could only stand and watch as Flynn kept crossing between me and the pig and I certainly wasn't going to get too close to an intelligent beast like that.

— *A Good Keen Man*

LLOYD SCOTT
(Scotty in the Toyota Commercials)

It's been nice being Scotty all these years. People forgot I was Lloyd Scott, the actor – I became the character in the commercials. They assumed I was a great friend of Barry Crump's and I was always getting people bowling up and asking me how he was. This happened even more in late 1980s when the ads were in full swing. Barry said the same thing: people would ask him when he'd last seen me and what I was up to.

Although I am not like Scotty at all, it's certainly never bothered me to be known as Scotty. I was happy with the way we were portrayed – they were good characters – the ads were creatively produced and it was a good product. It was something I wouldn't like to have missed out on.

People have even forgotten over the years that originally Scotty was a Toyota representative who sold Crumpy a ute. They'd followed as Scotty grew to admire Crump's sense of humour, his pragmatic values, the way Crumpy kept surprising him, and of course, where Crump could take a vehicle.

There's some irony, of course, that for me recognition as an actor came from being on television ads with Barry Crump rather than for all the work I've done on the stage, but I suppose that's the way of the world and that's the influence of the television medium. I almost had to turn down the opportunity of working with Barry, too, but it's funny how it worked out in my favour. I was lucky.

I'd been in a couple of commercials for a sheep drench called Nilverm, made by Silver Screen, which had been quite successful, and I guess the character was a bit like the character of Scotty they created for the Toyota commercials. So when Silver Screen asked if I was interested in doing a vehicle commercial, of course I was.

In that first one I played an extremely young-looking Toyota dealer delivering a red Toyota Hilux to Barry. When Crump said, "Come on, Scotty, let me drive you up to the house," Scotty had no idea what he was getting himself into.

We had no seat belts on and that became a bit of a controversial issue a bit later on, but they wanted it that way so we could get thrown around a bit and, boy, it really did throw me around. I landed in Barry's lap a couple of times and smacked my head several times on the roof of the cab as we drove up and down trying to say the words they had written for us at the same time as bouncing around the truck. Barry did all his own driving that day, although subsequently there were times neither of us was allowed in the truck during filming. I suppose they were a little bit worried what might happen.

That was my first experience of Barry. He was extremely affable, very open and easy to talk to and there was lots to talk to him about, of course, because of his background and the interesting things he had done. Having been an interviewer I found that I just kept asking questions and would listen rather than be a contributor myself.

He was with his wife Robyn when we first met. They were both Baha'i people and he talked a little about his Baha'i faith as we were driving out to the job in his Toyota. We got on fine and I think in some ways the real key to his popularity was that he made everybody feel like a friend. In the time that I knew him, certainly those early five or six years, it seemed that, wherever I went, everybody I met either knew him or had read his books or knew someone who knew him . . . they were just everywhere. He'd made this incredible impact on the country.

It was always interesting when Barry sang because sometimes the key wouldn't suit him and he wouldn't know whether to sing up high or down the bottom. He always sounded best singing down low with that wonderful voice of his, it was like a lorry starting. He'd pick it up and go with it and whatever parts he found difficult he'd just get through with the sound of his voice. And the thing that would make it work for viewers was realising that was Barry singing.

I was talking to the Toyota people and one of them said, "I remember once you came in and Barry had already arrived and he turned around and you gave each other a big hug. I was just amazed to see Barry Crump hugging another man, I was really impressed by that." As an actor I've always given people big hugs and that was how we always greeted each other.

He was very modest about both his writing and his acting. When we first got to work together he'd say to me, "Oh, I'm not an actor, Scotty, just push me around a bit." But he was always really willing to try things, he never said, "I can't be bothered with that", and he was always willing to listen to things you said. I suppose he was being Barry in the commercials but there was still an acting factor in it for him to come up with a result that the writers had written in.

It was hard keeping up with Barry. He moved about four times in the time that I knew him, to Opotiki, Wanaka, then up to Havelock South and finally to Tauranga and each time I found out through other people. All that time I'd lived in Wellington. If we'd lived closer, I'm sure we would have seen more of each other, but as it was we only saw each other when we worked together.

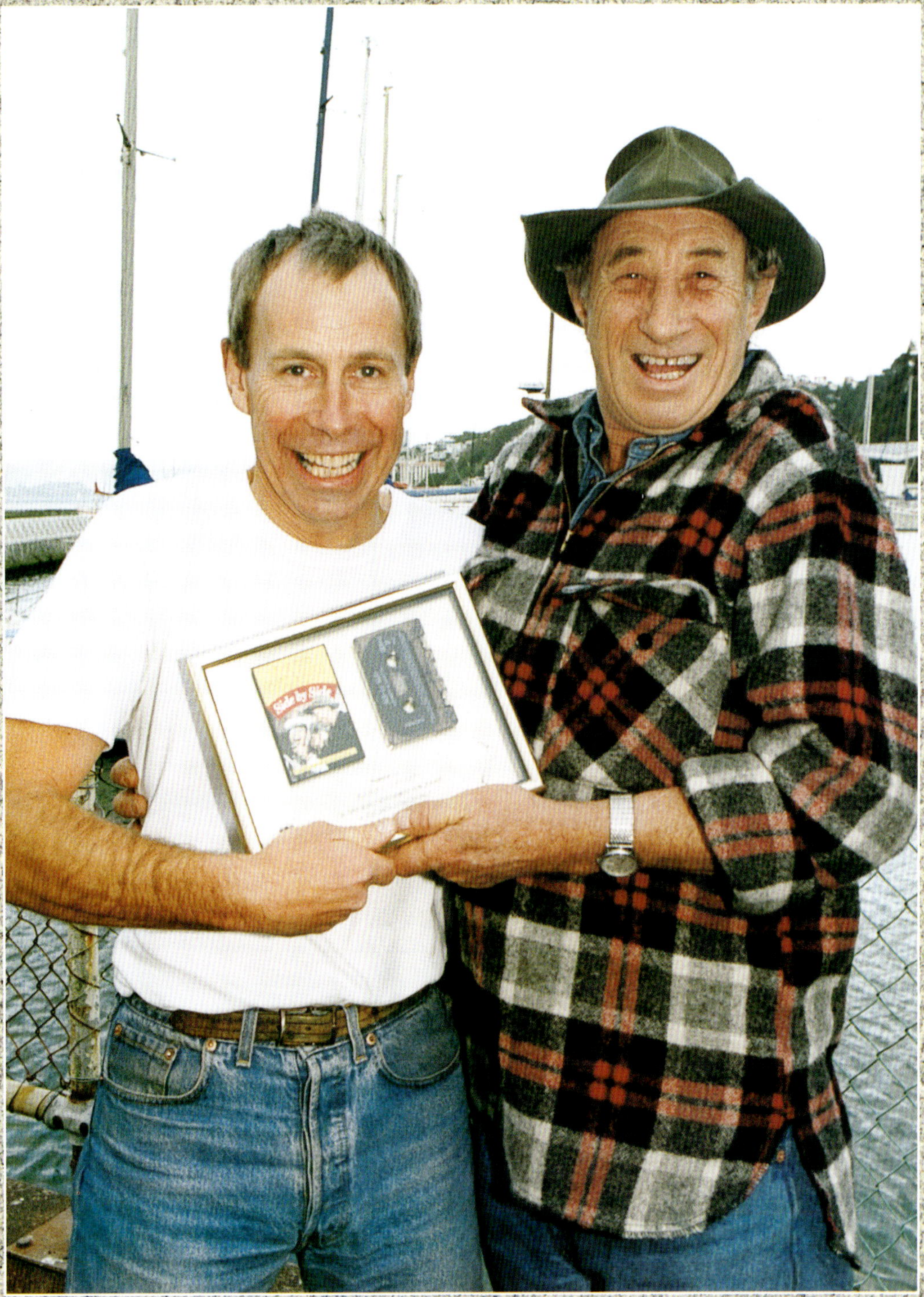
Side by Side

BOB FIELD
(Managing Director of Toyota New Zealand)

BARRY NEEDED A NEW SET OF WHEELS. HE'D SEEN A UTE ON THE SIDE OF THE ROAD WHICH HE LIKED THE LOOK OF WHEN HE WAS DRIVING PAST. HE CAME TO US AND SAID, "WHAT DO I NEED TO DO TO GET ONE OF THOSE?"

That was how the Toyota commercials came about, in total only eleven minutes of film but some of the most memorable made in this country.

At that time we wanted to promote Hilux, a very robust four-wheel-drive built locally, which we believed was an ideal vehicle for the New Zealand countryside. Barry Crump was the epitome of the off-road New Zealand rural scene, so it was a good fit. Scotty was brought in to provide a foil for Barry's larger-than-life character. The first ad went into production at the end of 1982 and screened in 1983, and we made the last of the eleven in 1995.

What appealed about them, I think, was that Barry was simply being himself and true to character and therefore all the more believable. They appealed even though some of the driving scenes were outrageous. It was always quite clear that there was distinct entertainment value in them and the driving was not intended to be taken literally as an endorsement of the vehicle's potential.

We had a few complaints about the driving, but not many. It's fair to say that if people tried to emulate the way Barry handled that ute it would be quite dangerous, but because the ads were so obviously humorous people didn't believe they were being offered a serious driving tip or being shown the best way of getting around the country.

We never encouraged Crump to try to act. He did try to sing, with not much success, but Scotty was a good coach. As a professional actor, Scotty brought out Barry's skills and, although he was originally there to play second fiddle to Barry, it certainly became an equal partnership. It was a credit to Barry that he allowed that to happen, that he shared the stage with Scotty and didn't feel intimidated by him. I think he respected Scotty for helping him through.

In the 1980s we put on quite a few black-tie social functions for dealers, fancy affairs with casts of thousands, and Barry would come along looking very uncomfortable in his dinner suit. He reckoned it was the first time he'd been in a dinner suit in his life. He would usually last the distance. The bow tie didn't stay straight, the cuffs were hanging down over his hands (he didn't know what cuff links were or he didn't have any) but he was sociable enough.

I think he got uncomfortable being in the city, and he found it a strain trying to be polite for too long on social occasions, so that was never expected a lot of him. He used to come to one-night conferences and enjoy them, but then he was quite happy to move on somewhere else.

He used to turn up to speak at dealer conferences – the sort of occasion where he'd cut himself a door in the wall with his chainsaw and push his way in, with the over-oiled chainsaw still roaring and smoking. He even sang on the odd occasion. Surprise appearances were always the most effective, and people's faces lit up when they saw him. He'd just stand up and say, "Gidday," and everyone would fall about laughing. It was quite extraordinary, he didn't actually have to say much. I guess that's a measure of the respect they had for him.

Barry used to use Toyota as a bit of a home, and he would ring in from time to time, not just to me but also to our marketing people. I think it was a relationship where we regarded him as part of our team and I think he regarded himself as part of that team too.

I respected Barry and I miss him. The relationship we had was a very close one, and we were very sad to say goodbye to him. He was a generous person who took his writing very seriously and if we've made a contribution to Barry's memory it's not just with the ads. I think it's that the relationship gave him the funding and the freedom to continue writing.

I told a story at the funeral which illustrated so many people's experience of how Barry Crump touched their lives. When I was in the fourth form I had a very traditional English teacher and we were filled up with Thomas Hardy and all sorts of English literature. Surprisingly, I won the essay prize and I chose Barry's second book, *Hang on a Minute Mate*, as my prize. The English teacher wouldn't hear of it and we had a head-on clash over it, but in the end I insisted and at prizegiving I was presented with the book wrapped in brown paper. It's an illustration of the fact that Barry's early writing was not accepted in literary circles, and that was quite painful for him because he took his writing seriously.

After the funeral someone came up to me, quite a rough diamond, and said that he'd learned to read in jail. He now went back to teach other prisoners to read and the only books that kept them interested were Barry Crump's. I just wonder how many people have started reading or got interested in reading through Barry Crump, people who'd otherwise look down their noses on reading as not interesting and a waste of time. But if Barry Crump – being the sort of guy he was – was writing books, they must be okay.

At Toyota we recognised that Barry was a special New Zealand icon and he would be able to preserve that uniqueness only if he was not over-used on television. For that reason we had an exclusive contract with him and you never saw him appear on any other advertising. It meant that Barry would be free to continue writing; we made it worthwhile to him and he preserved his integrity as a writer. And he had his wheels.

The commercial series went for twelve years and had a huge impact. I think the ads are classic and are probably the most successful television commercial series we've had or will ever have. But the commercials pale into insignificance compared to the contribution Barry Crump made to New Zealand writing and reading. He's sold more books than probably any other novelist, but you didn't hear Barry boasting or defending himself. He was a typical New Zealander in that respect, modest about his successes and taking criticism on the chin even when he hurt inside. We miss him. You can't replace a legend like that.

Toyota

Toyota in the Sheraton
Toyota in the mud
Toyota on the motorway
Or churning through the flood.

Toyota in the sandhills
Toyota in the town
Toyota parked in Dargaville
With people hanging round.

Toyota for a pack-horse
Toyota for a leap
Toyota for the open road
When everyone's asleep.

Listening to a western tape
The headlights on the line
We want to make the Ferry
And she sails at half past nine.

With a deer across the bull-bar
And a live one on the back
We boot her through the lupin
And make ourselves a track.

Toyota towing Henry's truck
Or humming through the Haast
Looking for a camping-place
We knew of in the past.

Free of spares and spanners
On easy roads and rough
I spin my new Toyota
From the North Cape to the Bluff.

CRAIG HOWAN
(Former Manager)

BARRY'S STRENGTHS WERE OBVIOUS AND BUSINESS ACUMEN WASN'T ONE OF THEM. HE PROBABLY EARNED A HELL OF A LOT OF MONEY IN HIS LIFE. IN THE TIME THAT I KNEW HIM HE EARNED A HELL OF A LOT MORE, BECAUSE I MADE sure he did. But he wasn't into money, he never wanted it, his comment about money was, "I don't worry about money and money doesn't worry me," and that's how it was. He'd got money off books over the years but never in major lump sums, just a few thousand dollars here and there. He never concerned himself with gain and when he had money he spent or gave it away.

I bought him a $20,000 tractor when he was living at Opotiki. He needed a tractor to do up the tracks so I got one for him, a four-wheel-drive with front-end loader. Barry loved it and used it a lot. "What did you do with the tractor?" I asked him when he left the farm at Opotiki, and he said, "Oh, I gave it to a neighbour." If somebody needed something, and he was in a position to give it to them, he would.

Opotiki was the first piece of land he ever owned. He'd been living there for some years on a block of land belonging to a friend. I think he got a sum from his first Toyota ad, and that was about the amount these people wanted for their piece of land, just a bare block with a shed on it, so he bought it.

The image of the good keen man grew and he carried it on and added to it, enhanced it and became it. He may not have been entirely that, he certainly wasn't entirely who he appeared to be. He was like every other human being, he could be outrageously ignorant, he could be outrageously loving, he could be everything.

He had an ability to store and retain all sorts of things and he had a great amount of energy. The light he shone on the people he touched was enough for every single one of them and that's why so many people remember him and were touched by him. But that light was still usually shaded and if he shone it directly on someone it was an honour and a privilege. Sometimes the light could be a little too bright for you.

He was a strong man who had an aura about him. You either have it or you don't, and he had it. He commanded an audience; he didn't always want to, he just did. He had the ability to write, he could tell jokes – he would never run out of jokes – he was a wonderful yarn teller. And he loved life, he believed life was an adventure and he was on one. He didn't conform to the rules of the rest of society. He had a wonderful life.

We used to call each other Brother.

Barry and I were living in a warehouse in Auckland when he met Maggie in a bar. She left her job to work on the book he was writing and they went to Wanaka and then Havelock for a couple of years. They bought my land at Welcome Bay from me.

We had our arguments, of course – you don't spend ten years with somebody without having one – but we never had a falling out. I lived a long time with him. It was a great shock to lose him. I'd always believed that a man with that sort of presence was never going to die.

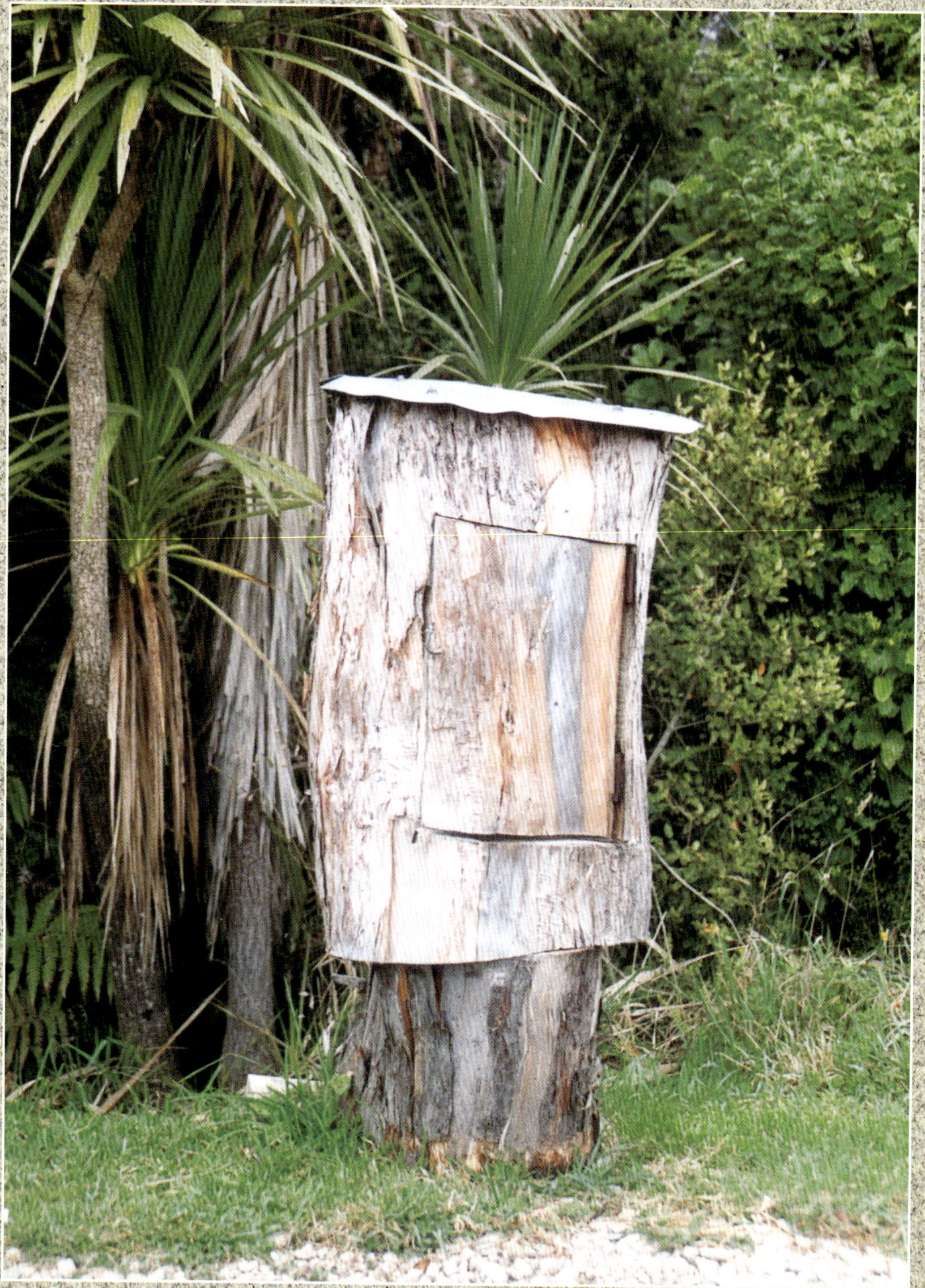

Chapter 6
From The Letterbox

You can tell a lot about someone by the box they put out at their front gate for the mail, and nothing expresses our ingenuity better than the good old Kiwi postbox. They can be as varied and individual as their makers . . . The amount of care taken in the construction of a postbox tells us something of the constructor. Some postboxes are carefully designed and built to receive regular hand-written airmail letters from friends and family, while others have obviously been knocked up by people who never write letters and never receive anything but bills, bad news and brochures.

– Forty Yarns and a Song

ANDORRA,
(Between Spain and the South of France in the Pyrenees Mts)

Dear Bryce*

Too many adventures to tell you about in a letter. Been thinking about you and hoping things are going okay for you. Herewith a token of our esteem; a crazy smoke-lighter. It goes best in a wind. You insert the burnt end of the wick into the end of the tube opposite the rowell until it sticks out the top. Then stroke the wheel. Nothing will happen at first, but an inspection will reveal that there's a flint in the thing. This can be made to actually strike sparks onto the wick by running along holding the wheel against the side of the building. Sometimes this is not necessary and the sparks fly with the mere flick of your thumb and spray onto the wick, which will then refuse to ignite. This can be overcome by touching the end of a lighted cigarette to the wick and blowing gently. The wick will glow steadily,

at the same time giving off a smell like the burning of a chronic bed-wetter's kapok mattress. This tends to clear some of the less experienced members of the gathering away on other business and you are then free to pass one round. And here a hint that may save you some rather unsettling spasms of anguish: Always be the one slinging the 'lighter', because the poor bugger who stokes her up off the Spanish Special (Ronsono!) cops a lungful of smog that causes every pore on his body to clang suddenly shut like a porthole, his eyes redden, bulge and water, he clutches his throat, doubles up and falls wheezing onto the sofa. DON'T TOUCH HIM! He's all right – simply remove the smoke from between his nerveless fingers (he won't mind) and pass it on round. By the time it gets back to him he'll most likely be starting to come round and a man of courage should be back into it in no time.

You will have noticed by this time that there is a cap attached to the burning end of the wick. This hooks into the wick and caps the tube, extinguishing the flow. But don't worry about the cap. Within two days it will have been lost. They fall off. It doesn't matter; you simply pull the wick back into the tube when you want to put it out, place your thumb over the end and it will go out immediately. Another hint in the use of your new lighter is to turn the wick as you push it through the tube. This makes it possible. The flints are standard and spare metres of wick can be obtained by sending a 35-peseta postal-note to Senor D. Quixote, Medina 35326968 (or was it 34326968?), Madrid. Failing this you may have some success in whittling down a tampax and soaking it in candle-grease. Though it's unlikely that one would ever be able to match the acrid pungency of the genuine Spanish article. It's taken them hundreds of years of eating nothing but sardines and olive oil to get themselves immune to the stench of those wicks, and some of the pongs we've encountered here and there were certainly not produced overnight.

However, if you follow the instructions carefully you should get many weeks of frustration and excitement from your new lighter.

Be seeing you,

Our love to you and all our friends,

Barry

*Bryce Peterson (see Chapter 4).

RAROTONGA
(WHERE THE FRUIT THAT GOES IN THE BOWL IS ACTUALLY GROWN!)
SABBATH

Dearly-loved Lorna, highly-esteemed Steph, deeply-admired Scott, and sadly-missed Matty,[*]

It was a real stir in the camp to hear from – wait on, wasn't there someone else in your gang? Oh yes, Alex (sorry about that) – you all. Couldn't sleep last night from thinking about you all, plus the fact that forty-one vegetarian dogs were bewailing their ill-nourishment, some of the locals had found a bottle of beer and threw an uninhibited party on the spot, which happened to be in the coconut trees outside our window, a boatload of people from one of the outer islands ran through their drumming-act repertoire on the beach of the lagoon out the front for their Constitution-week item, and Tupuhi finally got his mufflerless two-stroke going about eleven-thirty and apparently decided he'd get as many rev vvvvvs out of it as he could before it broke down again, and Makiriri had a difference with his cousin Kura and decided to come and live with us forever (he went home this morning). An average sort of an evening for here.

I've cut two reports out of the paper since we've been here with the idea of sending to someone who'd appreciate them, but we can't find them. One tells of a young lady who stole a green skirt from a house! The court was gravely concerned and reserved their decision for a few days in order to ponder this weighty matter. The other was headlined Vandalism at Titikaveka! and informed the stunned population that someone had thrown a stone through the window of a bus that was parked outside the Roman Catholic Church (it wasn't us!) at the time. The police were thoroughly investigating this wanton act of vandalism. No kidding!

This would have to be the most violence-free place on earth. The people here are an inspiration. There are children everywhere, and we haven't seen one piece of bad behaviour yet. The only time I've seen a youngster cry was when young Tiromi ran into the edge of the door with his head the other day, though apparently a baby cried when Robyn was holding it because young Tara was still laughing about it yesterday.

The Baha'i Assembly in Auckland sent us here to show the Baha'is on one of the outer islands how the administration order works and we haven't even got there yet, but the idea of us teaching these people anything only makes me feel humble whenever I think of it. Don't know how long we'll be here, we'll probably run out of money in a month or so. Our van's in a shed at brother Bill's and we'll probably waft down your direction when the wind is in the right quarter. We're not really trying to avoid you, you know.

I've been writing a book called Don't Call Me Shorty in conditions I wouldn't have believed. It's not the drums and shouting and running through the house so much as them coming to ask me if I know where Taata is, or can they borrow the pen, or have some paper – and it doesn't interrupt me somehow. The book's about a short bloke who's real good-natured excepting when anyone makes remarks about his height. Then he can't help himself. He gets keen on golf and . . . I'll write a bit of it down to give you an idea (It'll help fill up the page!).

Start of excerpt: The second slightly-embarrassing thing that happened was when I was waiting at the Kelston Golf-club to meet the Colonel for a game . . . and the slightly-embarrassing thing itself was simply that I got caught sneaking a bar-stool out of the club-house. Nothing very serious in itself, I'd have thought, but three blokes bailed me up and demanded to know if there was any reason why they shouldn't call the police and lay charges of attempted theft against me.

I told them the truth but they didn't seem to want to believe me. So I went through it again for them.

"The golf pro at the Mount Carlon club, who also happens to be a personal mate of mine, told me that when you take your stance for a golf swing your legs should be slightly-bent at the knees, just as though you were sitting on a bar-stool. You can ring him up and ask him if you like. I was just borrowing this stool here to try it out with."

And their story was that if a short-arse like me sat on that stool my feet wouldn't even reach the ground.

I hadn't thought of that, I admit, but that was no reason for them to start making insulting remarks about the way a man was built, and I wasn't going to stand there and let this flat-footed, big-bummed, blubber-gutted, nail-biting, round-shouldered, bullet-headed, false-toothed, half-bald, trouble-hunting understudy to a maggot call me a short-arse and get away with it, and that goes for his big-nosed, shrivel-eared, narrow-eyed, bony-knuckled, calcium-deficient, cheaply-dressed, knock-kneed mate as well.

I was just getting ready to start on the third one when he lumbered off to call the police and have me removed from the club for causing a disturbance. They were out of their depth at insult-slinging and had to call in reinforcements.

I removed myself, thank you.

Fair puts a bloke off, that sort of thing. I was miles down the road when I suddenly remembered I was supposed to meet the Colonel. Nothing I could do about it now though. I certainly wasn't going back there again. I don't get along too well with people who make nasty remarks about other people's height.

End of excerpt.

And that sort of thing.

Robyn [Robin Lee Robinson] had just decided to change the spelling of her name. She reckons that if even the Kings haven't got it right she's (hang on, she's just stuck a freshly picked paw-paw in front of me) Ahhhhh! I like that stuff! Now, where was I – yes, well it seems that she's been having it mis-spelt all the way down the line and your letter was the last straw. She's given up and now wishes to be known to us all as RobIn.

Funny you should mention that you were toying with the idea of keeping Lorna on for another season, Alex. Just the other day the same idea occurred to me regarding RobIn. Haven't said anything definite about it yet, though.

No plans about your wonderful offer of that house, Alex. It looks as though we're destined to wander around, without roots, always being shifted by an unkind fate just as soon as we make friends somewhere, deprived of the homely comforts that other families gather about them over the years, doomed to live out our transient lives in a restless, wandering search that carries us ever . . . (Starting to get carried away again. The page is too big!) Anyway we think we should lovingly decline your offer, rather than risk causing you hassles over our uncertain future movements. We know it was a sincere and very generous gesture, Alex, and we're both just as grateful for it as though we'd been able to take you up on it.

We've both been most impressed by the King handwriting! By comparison mine's like the tracks of a drunken fowl, and Robin's is little better. Sloppy.

The big thing that's been happening around here is that a short time before the annual float-parade scene (a week of great festivity) the local Baha'is decided to stick a float in. We've been busy, but with everyone getting stuck in it was a hunk of fun, really. It was by far the best float in the parade. And to top it off the judges put us exactly where we wanted to be, second prize. (Gave us the same notice as the winner without causing any resentment.) One bloke had to make a cut-out replica of the sun with God written on it, and he made a metre-round papier-mache globe, painted it gold. Put GOD in raised letters of crumpled tinfoil. Someone else painted signs for the side and back of our little truck – the house has suddenly filled up with people, music, coconut and oranges. I asked a young girl "When do you do all your dancing here?" and she said, "When we hear music." (Ask a silly question . . . !) – anyway, the float. We found a 9-foot square side of a packing case that fitted in. A couple of us fitted a length of pipe sticking up in the middle. We fixed the golden globe on the top of the pipe with golden ropes coming off it and on the ropes were oval golden discs with Moses, Christ, Mohammed, Krishna, Buddha and Baha'ullah painted on in black. Then the local ladies descended on the truck and completely covered it from road to roof, windscreen, door, front, with greenery. Then they stuck borders of flowers and ferns and stuff around the edges and covered the deck with yellow petals. In the meantime other women were getting six youngsters dressed up in Arab kind of gear and the Baha'i float fronted up with the six boys, each holding a golden rope with the name of one of the religions descending from the big golden globe walking slowly around, the globe turning with them, and signs on the side surrounded with flowers saying that God, mankind, and religions are all one. With a beautifully-woven square on the front with the word BAHA'I woven in raised – Hell, running out of space, love to all!

*The King family - Alex, Lorna, Stephanie, Scott and Matty. Variously addressed in the following letters as Your Highnesses, Your Eminences, O Kings (See Chapter 4).

OPOTIKI, BAY OF PLENTY

O Kings,

A flood of Sardanapalian regardancy fills our hearts and thrills our souls as we take up our pen in reply to your wonderful message of love, coming as it did so close on the heels of your money-no-object phone call. We're unworthy . . .

Where to start – the adventure of the crazy dog, no; the log that came down in the big flood and wiped . . . no, not noteworthy enough to pass on. There was the helicopter crash on our . . . no, but there was the visit from – no, you'd only think we were big-noting. Robyn suggests we tell you about her recent academic achievements and our adoption of . . .

There's been a considerable pause here for a rather heated family consultation on what's worth mentioning and what's not. I mean, the bloody woman'd have all our friends think we were a bunch of bloody – blast it, she won't even let me put that!

However, we did get that other business fixed up okay, though we haven't decided what we're going to do with the money yet. (I had intended here to include a diagram of my operation, but an altercation ensued regarding the number of stitches and the position and actual length of the incision, so the whole thing ended up in the fire.)

Anyway, there's nothing to stop me telling you about our trip to Japan, only we didn't actually get away in the finish. We did get our passports brought up-to-date and our international driving licences.

Another slight altercation has ensued. It started with me deciding to mention our invitation from the minister and lasted for two days. We've finally agreed on something, though. We've agreed that we'd better try to get this letter finished today some time so we can post the books back when I go into town tomorrow to receive the award (sneaked that one in).

So, as you can see, we're still getting on okay. By clinging to the example set us so long ago by your good selves, we continue to live in matrimonial harmony and bliss, and if Lorna ever starts complaining about being chained up under the house or going crook about the tucker – don't worry. I'll just dash off a book called Cast Lambs and Castor-oil to make her feel all right about it. No, don't thank me, it's the least a man . . . What? Oh no! I'd better go and let Robyn off for a run, the whimpering's distracting me a bit. She can make a hell of a mess if you don't . . . she's digging this big hole by the corner of . . . undermining the porch. No gratitude.

**Love to all,
Winter smiles,**

Barry

OPOTIKI, BAY OF PLENTY
Mundy

Dear Alex, Lorna and Further Issue!
Thankx for the foters, the book (The Life and Times of a Good Keen Man) is finished and we're now putting the photographs to it. I was actually short of a photo of myself as a youngster, your one will do admirably and only those in the know will ever know it's a ring-in. Then, when things get to the bottom of the barrel for you you'll be able to expose the whole rotten scandal to the Sunday papers for a large undisclosed sum and live happily ever after. The things a bloke goes through to make sure his mates will be okay in their dotage!

Me little farm is just about completed. The fences are all done, the road is metalled from one end to the other, the house renovated, the bridge redecked, new tractor shed, woman and child in good hick and humour – even the water in the river outside is fresh (in fact it's been in flood for a month or more!) – all things set for a happy, contented and secure future. The place has cost me $150,000, not counting sweat, so I've stuck it on the market for $95,000 negotiable and am preparing to hit the road again. Can't handle things too easy. Craig [Howan] and I are buying some incredibly expensive video gear and intend making some wholesome TV material around the country.

So the times of arab horses, border collie dogs, tortoiseshell cats and coloured women are over. Wonder what the next adventure will bring. It'll almost certainly bring me down your way in the not-too-distant.

I've enclosed these photos as proof of my honest and hard-working nature. Please don't return them, it'd only confuse me.

I've got to go and do some filming on Wednesday and I've lost my false teeth somewhere. That'll be interesting!

They're making a feature film of one of my books and we're battling to eliminate the filthy language and sex they've written into the script. They can't help themselves. What have we come to.

Breakfast wafts, then I'll feed the animals and maybe go in for a few holes of golf with Craig. What a life!

Warmest love to all,
Barry Crump

PS Some relatives have done a trace of our family tree and I find that my name is not Crump, but Cramp. My actual name is John Barrie Cramp. I hereby deny all responsibility for any questionable behaviour by the Crump bloke in your area.
Signed,
Johnny Cramp

COLLINGWOOD
P.O. Golden Bay
Wednesday or Thursday

Q: What do you call an elephant with no ears?
A: Anything you like – he can't hear you.

Dearest Kings!

Just back from a trip to the far north, loaded to the gunnels with gifts, encrusted with medals, festooned with awards, ears still ringing with bullshit, reeling from arrangements, overwhelmed with offers, wrinkled, rumpled, red-eyed and ragged-out – so to get your letter was a special delight, apart from some slight embarrassment connected with gifts left under caravan beds. (Gets you right THERE, mate!) Thump, cough, cough.

Whilst browsing through a friend's shop in Kerikeri the other day a name leapt out of the glitter and jumble and struck us as familiar. "I know that name!" I said. "Me too," said Robyn.

Well, after much cogitation and discussion we finally hit on it. "It's a King name!" cried Robyn. "So it is," I said. And that's how we remembered your happy smiling faces in that remote corner of the globe. We regret to have to report that they'd missed out on Alex and Lorna. Enquiries revealed that those names were – What? Okay, I was only trying to . . . Robyn says she's got something important to say, so I'll just Ouch! Okay, okay, take the bloody typewriter.

Barry

WANAKA POST OFFICE
April

Your Highnesses!

Greetings from the Land of the Golden Poplar and The Shrunken Sheep (The Merino once stood five feet at the shoulder but the wily swede-eaters in the Land of the Rumpty Romney, jealous of the wealth of the worthy wool-growers to their west, bribed the Wicked Witch of Winton to concoct a convocation against us, and she sent a magpie, trained to utter a spell that would shrink the Mighty Merino to the size of one of their wretched woollies, but the stupid magpie forgot one of the ardles in its warble and the spell failed to shrink the skin of the Merino, thus giving our shearers no end of trouble . . .)

But I digress – I return herewith the document you so kindly committed to my care, which has been of great value. How else could this humble and uneducated scribe have guessed that a transistorised transmitter and receiver circuit in the electronic housing was coupled to a transmitter and receiver antenna network concealed in the search head; and that when all this was energised an electromagnetic field was developed around the transmitting coil; and that the receiving oil was inductively balanced to the transmitting coil; and that when a ferrous or non-ferrous object was introduced into the electromagnetic field an unbalanced condition resulted, which the receiver coil interpreted and registered on a meter or in a speaker – or both? I would never have known that such wondrous things took place within the white man's glorious gadget!

My worthy scribblings have been inestimably enhanced by the acquisition of this esoteric information, and posterity is undoubtedly indebted to Your Highnesses' gracious generosity in entrusting me with this massive missive!

Word has reached us that Your Highnesses are soon to visit this corner of your Kingdom on some high purpose, and we look forward to seeking an audience with you on that occasion. In the meantime keep your heads down and your strides on and don't let any bastard put one across you.

I remain, your humble and obedient servant,

Crump

WARD 6, WANAKA INFIRMARY
Tuesday (I think)

Dear Alex, Lorna and further issue – Your Eminences,
　I feel I owe you some explanation for having failed to return these photographs I borrowed from you for a week in nineteen eighty-six. I hasten to assure you that the reason for this outrageous breach of etiquette lies not in any deliberate neglect of responsibility on my part. On the contrary, my attempts to return these photos to you have taken me to the brink of a nervous breakdown, a serious domestic crisis, and bankruptcy (the result of counselling and damages charges). Only I and my Maori psychologist know the anguish I have been through over what have become known to us as 'Te Whoters O Te Kingi', TWOTK for short.
　You may remember, Your Eminences, that in the year of the Lesser Crested Grebe I bought a camera and began to assemble my collection of Humble Abodes, which was subsequently made into a calendar. In the course of this I discovered that one must take a large number of photographs to get a few good ones. (Out of five hundred photos I couldn't find twelve that were suitable for my calendar and had to use one from my Postbox Collection.) Add to this my collection of Fence Posts, my series of Tree Stumps and my mossy Rocks, Clothes Lines, Signs, Old Tractors, Boots, Headstones, Bridges and Bird Nests. I ended up with more than six thousand photographs stored in boxes in the spare room.
　Then one day when we had visitors the kids got into the photos and shuffled them into a state of hopeless disorder. Photos and negatives inextricably confused, and your ones were mixed up amongst them.
　I began to sort through the mess in order to find your photos so I could return them to you, but soon discovered that after going through a few hundred photos I'd forgotten which ones I was looking for. It took me three months to recover three of them, by the end of which time I'd become a nervous wreck. I began raving in my sleep, sitting bolt upright and calling on the gods to reveal the whereabouts of those precious photographs, and scaring the daylights out of my wife.
　This resulted in me being eventually banished from the nuptial bedchamber. The spare room being filled with photographs, I was forced to sleep thereafter in the cab of the ute, and in the throes of a nightmare in which I was drowning in a river of photographs I kicked the vehicle out of gear and it rolled away down the hill, wiped out the clothes line, bowled the long-drop and crashed through the fence into the neighbour's fowl house.
　The insurance company didn't believe my story about the photographs and refused to pay out, leaving me with a six-thousand-dollar bill for the damage and a suspicious, embittered neighbour.

I consulted a doctor who told me I was run-down and put me on a course of Librium and sleeping-pills. This made me very dopey, so he added Methamphetamine to the others, which took away my appetite, so he prescribed Havakai Capsules, which caused me to break out in birthmarks, accompanied by severe horripilation.

My recollection of subsequent events is hazy. I am informed that I was found sitting on a gatepost in pouring rain, engaged in an intense contemplation of my forefinger and muttering "twotk, twotk". It was then that I was taken to the Maori psychologist, who sent me to a hypnotherapist, who diagnosed that I was suffering from a deep-seated lack of self-confidence, brought about by an exaggerated sense of responsibility over some photographs.

During the long months of recuperation, whenever I felt strong enough, I would take a few dozen photographs and sift through them in the search for the ones I'd borrowed from you. I've found these nine and still have more than three thousand photos to go through. I cherish hopes of finding the other three over the next two or three years.

I humbly apologise for any inconvenience over this inexcusable delay in returning your property to you.

Respectfully yours,

B Crump (Introvert)

HAVELOCK 10TH

Lorna dear,*

We were deeply disturbed to hear that you'd been a bit off your oats, and we look forward to news of your complete recovery.

Nothing much happening up here. I do a bit of riting and Maggie lives in the garden. Most days when the weather's okay we launch our little boat at the head of Pelorus Sound (1 minute from home) and go fishing or exploring, or hunting for the elusive Pungapeople who live out there in the Sound and get up to most of the mischief. How about coming up and giving us a hand to catch one. We'd be famous!

I've just finished writing the enclosed pome (I strongly deny that the character of Tanglewood is based on Alex).

**Our thoughts and prayers are with you, dear.
Regards to Alex, Scott, Matty and Steph.**

Love from Crumpy, Maggie and Anton.

*Following news of Lorna's major illness

WANAKA POST OFFICE (FOR NOW)
Wednesday

O Kings,[*]

a brief note to express our heartfelt sympathies in this time of trouble and anxiety for you all. We can only hope and pray that Steph comes through okay. Tell her not to worry too much about the loss of balance, it's happened to me lots of times. Something to do with drinking on an empty stomach, I'm told.

It pleases these subjects to learn that you are busily and gainfully employed. There is nothing worse than a King cabbaging around with his head in a bag of glue, or lying back on cushions puffing on a hookah. The chunder boat looks great and I like your trailer. Mass production!

Of course you can let them publish my letters in the local paper. I have used one of them myself in a book, though your name has been changed to Fred.

We now set sail for the Marlborough Sounds and a new adventure.

Our prayers for you all, and especially Stephanie.

(Crumpy)

Crumpy, Maggie and Anton.

[*] Following news that Stephanie had a brain tumour

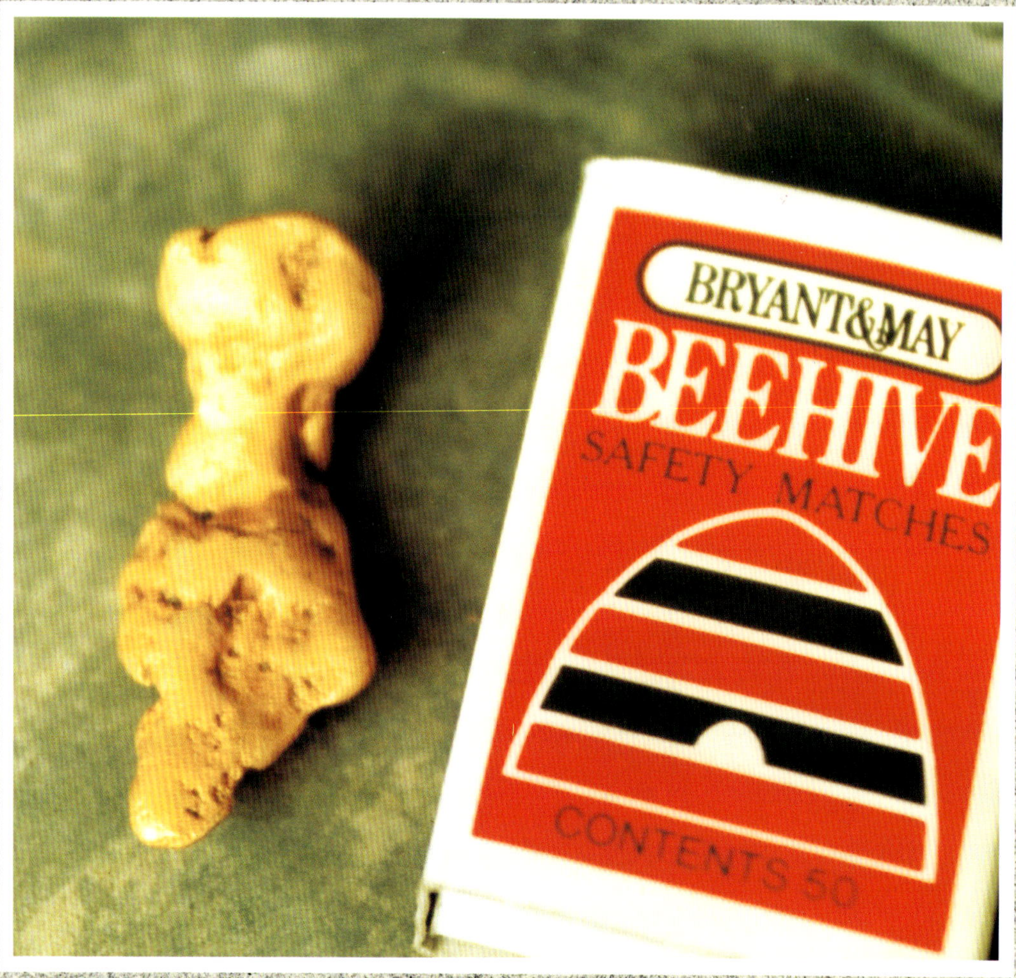
BRYANT&MAY
BEEHIVE
SAFETY MATCHES
CONTENTS 50

THE NUGGET OF THE TATTOOED LEG
Wanaka Post Office Otago

Dear Alex, Lorna, and that which has issued from the Royal loins. Greetings from this far-flung corner of the kingdom!

You would think from the enclosed photographic evidence that my years of prospecting and deprivation in mountain and valley have finally paid off, but you yourselves as miners from way back know that gold is strange stuff and causes people to do strange things, and I came upon this nugget in the strangest way. I feel impelled to pass on to you the details surrounding this strange event.

I was in Queenstown one night a few weeks back, hastening to an assignation with a Nepalese drug dealer. The directions I'd been given took me through the Haitian quarter and, glancing around at the squalid hovels of this crowded sprawling slum, I shuddered and raised my coat collar against the clammy late-night mist and hurried on my way, anxious to do my business and to be away from this unwholesome place.

Suddenly, up ahead of me on a dimly-lit street corner, I saw three men attacking another. I immediately ran to his assistance and, by the use of some karate skills I'd learned while tea picking on the Chathams, I managed to fend off the three huge Negro attackers, who finally gave up and ran off into the darkness.

Turning for the first time to the man I'd saved I saw that he was an old Chinese gentleman, lying in a crumpled heap on the littered roadway. He appeared to be badly hurt. I gently lifted him up and carried him into a nearby hovel and laid him on an evil-smelling couch of cured goatskins, and ordered the trembling Vietnamese occupants to bring towels and hot water.

By the dim light of a flickering lamp I removed the old man's filthy shirt and washed him. He was badly bruised and had several knife cuts about his body. I cleaned his wounds and staunched them with bandages improvised from a burnoose torn into strips. Then I forced a few drops of Fanta between his clenched gums and laid him back on the couch and covered him with a dog-skin blanket. After a while the Fanta began to take its effect and the poor old man drifted off into a troubled sleep.

I sat with him through the long night, mopping the sweat from his fevered brown and checking his pulse and breathing, and towards morning he woke and began mumbling feverishly. I bent closer to try and hear what he was going on about and distinctly heard him say '"gold" and "map". Gold and map – at the mention of those magic words I was transmogrified, from a decent bloke doing another bloke a favour, to a miserable, mercenary, materialistic, misfeasant, misanthropist.

I shook him. "What gold?" I said urgently.

"Gold" he muttered "gold".

"Where?" I demanded.

"Map," he said, and fell weakly back against the sack of mussels I'd given him for a pillow.

I shook him again. "Where's the map?" I said.

"Leg," he muttered, "on my leg."

I threw aside the dog-skin blanket and slit his trouser leg with my knife and held the lamp closer, and there on the calf of his leg was a faded tattoo, a map giving directions to a spot in a creek deep in the Gore Mountains.

Taking the leg with me, I made my way back to my camp, and the next day I trekked into the mountains with my faithful burrow and prospecting equipment. Following the directions on the leg I picked my way through gorge and gully until, on the third day, I came to the spot marked on the leg.

I noticed a pile of stones that had once been built up into a cairn, so I dug there and to my horror unearthed a human skeleton in a shallow grave. The skull had been crushed in, telling of some grizzly deed perpetuated in the past.

"Probably over gold," I mused to myself, and just then I saw the gleam of gold among the bones of the skeleton's hand. It was the nugget in the enclosed photograph. I grabbed it and after gazing upon it for a while I put it in my pocket and then threw the bones aside and put the whole area through my riffle-box. But not another speck of gold did I find.

I could have murdered that old chink. He's put me crook. But it just goes to show you what men will do for "the muck called gold".

I'm happy to be able to report, however, that some good has come from that experience. Maggie and I have decided to shut ourselves away in the Ben Lomond shearers' quarters and spend our declining years working on a cure for gold fever. Doctor Crump's famous gold fever pills!

At the moment we're working on a mixture of sandflies bites, wet arses, numb fingers and nothing in the wash-up. If we can get that into a pill we feel that we will have made a break-through in the search for a remedy for this most degrading of human afflictions. Who knows what it might lead to? One of them Nobel prizes wouldn't go astray, or a seat on the Board (I've always wanted one of those), or maybe even an interview on the Holmes Show!

But enough of this day-dreaming, I must away and give Maggie a hand. She's having trouble getting the flavouring right. We've decided on a sardine-on-toast flavour for our pills.

So until we next meet, our warmest love to all.

Barry, Maggie and Anton

P.S.   You didn't think we'd tell you where we really got it, did you?

THE NUGGET OF THE TATTOOED LEG
August 1994

Oh Kings!

An epistle has reached this outpost, brought to us by our faithful runners in a cleft stick, informing us of your safe return from the far-flung corners of the Kingdom. We hadn't heard from you since receiving the photograph of your travelling entourage and had consulted Sir Tuppeny O'Sullivan, the eminent Ngai Tahu Tohunga, and on his advice burnt a candle at both ends in support of our ardent prayers for your safe return. We rejoice to have you back with us.

There have been developments in the mystery surrounding the nugget of the tattooed leg. Ever since our acquisition of this dysphoric bauble we have suffered a series of terrible calamities.

Our great aunt Bertha, after a lifetime of pious chastity, has taken to prostitution and when last heard of had stowed away on a Russian trawler. My brother's wife, on being diagnosed as having Mad Cow Disease, ran away to Surfers Paradise with the neighbour's Hereford bull. My other brother's eleven year old daughter got hold of his credit card and poured the whole family fortune into the pokey machine at the Arthurs Point pub. My brother-in-law has become schizophrenic and the last report we had of him was that he'd paid his income tax twice. Maggie has taken up Transcendental meditation and sits cross-legged for many hours each day on the top of Mount Barker, meditating on the various philosophies and religions of the world, whilst engaging in an ecstatic contemplation of her navel. I think she's become introverted. And now my dog is acting strange.

It's all become too much of a burden for me and I can no longer keep the secret of the accursed nugget of the tattooed leg to myself. Accordingly I reveal its origin to your eminences. The truth is enshrined in the enclosed booklet. I trust you will treat the information therein with discretion, in the interests of maintaining harmony and order in the Realm.

Inexpressibly Unburdened,
I remain, Your Humble And Obedient Servant,
John B Cramp, Esquire,
Barker Station,
Otago.

(Love, Barry and Maggie)

THE NUGGET OF THE TATTOOED LEG
Wanaka Post Office, Wanaka
3 October 1994

O Kings!

The saga of the nugget of the tattooed leg continues apace. The latest development took place during my quotidian post-prandial stroll through the streets of Arrowtown. I found myself in the Chinese quarter and, following an impulse, I decided to visit one of the pakapoo dens, which abound in that district.

I entered the portals of a false-fronted establishment called, of all things!, The Golden Nugget. At the far end of a sleazy bar a giant of a man guarded a curtained doorway. A man a little like you yourself to look at, Alex. Shaven head and bulging neck, flattened forehead, slitted eyes and pockmarked face. He stood there with his huge tattooed arms folded across his sagging breasts. I walked straight up to him and muttered a few words in flawless Cantonese that had been taught me by a member of a triad whom I'd befriended while working under-cover for The Bay Collection Agency in a Moroccan mental asylum. The esoteric words produced a magical effect and I was immediately ushered down a narrow stairway and into a dimly lit basement, where a number of figures were crouched intently over several pakapoo tables.

I took my place at one of the tables opposite a fat inscrutable oriental gent who was betting with wads of hundred dollar notes. My wife's car had been sold that day and I was carrying a large amount of cash with me. I took the money from my pocket and placed it on the table in front of me, and we began to play. Before long the stakes were too high for the other players and only the oriental gent and I were left at the table.

I remember the scene as though it was still happening. The five thousand dollars on the table, fairly evenly divided between the two of us, the dim light from the naked bulb, the air thick with the sickly smell of opium. The dealer, a huge negress wearing only a loin cloth and a green eye-shade deals the cards. My hand is good. My opponent glances at his cards and leaves them face down on the table and then pushes a wad of notes forward. A thousand dollars. I match it. He pushes forward another thousand. He has to be bluffing. I match him again.

Soon all the money is in the middle of the table. The room grows silent as the other gamblers leave their games and press around our table to watch. He pushes the last of his notes into the pile in the centre of the table. I've gone too far to pull out now. I reach into the concealed pocket in my waistcoat and bring out the nugget of the tattooed leg. It drops onto the table with a loud clunk.

A ripple of excitement runs through the room. For the first time the face of my opponent betrays emotion. He leans forward and with his eyes fixed on the nugget gleaming wickedly in the dim light, he says,

"Where you get this nugget?"

"Scrubby gully," I tell him. "Now ante up or show us your hand, sport."

"This nugget of tattooed leg," he states, unable to conceal the naked greed on his countenance.

"Show us your hand, pal," I say.

Suddenly he reaches into his inside coat pocket and brings out a document and places it on the table beside the nugget. I pick it up and read it. It's the deeds to a fifty-five foot motor boat. A photograph of the vessel is attached with a paperclip to the top left hand corner of the document. It looks okay to me. I fold the paper and put it back beside the nugget.

I'm swept, I have to show my hand.

I turn over a king.

He turns over an ace.

I turn over an ace.

He turns over a king.

I turn over my last card, another ace.

He turns over the table and all hell breaks loose. I grab at the nugget and the boat deeds as they slide towards me and dive for the door, stuffing them into my pocket. Behind me there's a frantic scramble going on for the money. At the top of the stairs my way is blocked by the huge Chinese guard. I catch him in the crutch with a karate kick from Karachi. He's a eunuch. I dig him in the solar plexus with my stiffened fingers, my hand sinks into a mattress of fat. I chop him across the side of his neck with the heel of my hand, a blow I once felled a bolting horse with. He has no neck. By this time his huge hand is reaching out for me. I make a desperate dive between his legs and scrabble out onto the street and make my way home, where I seat myself in front of the fire with the evening paper, a glass of sherry, my inextinguishable briar and my faithful spaniel's head resting on my slippered foot.

And that's how we came to be captain and first mate of a fifty-five foot boat moored in Picton. We move on board later in October and prepare to explore the Marlborough Sounds. We shall continue our reports from that region.

One last thing, Your Highnesses, you'll understand I know. It's just that my wife thinks I bought the boat with her car money. I'd appreciate if you'd keep the true facts surrounding the acquisition between ourselves. Domestic harmony and all that. I'd actually promised to give up gambling and my wife mightn't understand.

Our next epistle will probably have a nautical flavour. We'll advise you of our new address and phone number.

Until we meet,
We remain,
Your Humble and Obedient Servants,
The Crumps

6 JANUARY 1994

Dear Barry Crump

With all our heart we congratulate you on your New Year Honour, but more than that thank you for writing your books. We have a fourteen-year-old son who had NEVER read a book up until November of '93. He is dyslexic and goes to a Speld teacher.

We have taken him out of school and help him at home with the correspondence school programme. He got this book of yours about the bush and hunting, wow he read it in a week and his eyes sparkled, unbelievable.

For his birthday he wanted a slug gun, so we paid some and he had to work to get the rest, so milked the cows for two weeks and got his gun. His other desire was to go bush. He went into the national park by Opotiki, for three days hunting deer, they never saw one, but just enjoyed tramping in the bush and making the most of the outdoor life, so he was right into what you write about, could understand the words.

We found your book A Good Keen Man in a book exchange, so got it for him for Christmas, thinking he would read it and exchange it for another, but he wants to keep the books, another miracle, as the only things he ever kept were Murray Ball's picture books

Thanks again Barry for the opening up of a new world for him.

Love

Anne T. for Paul

"People handling dyslexics or difficult-to-teach kids have written me letters that are thoroughly heart-warming. More heart-warming than hearing you've sold 20,000 copies."

GOVERNMENT HOUSE
New Zealand

20th Dec. 1993.

Dear Mr Crump

I am writing to advise you that Her Majesty The Queen has been pleased to award you the honour of Member of the Civil Division of the Most Excellent Order of the British Empire (MBE) in recognition of your services to New Zealand.

The honour is to be announced in the New Year Honours 1994 which will be officially announced from 6 am on Friday 31 December 1993.

As you will appreciate this information should be kept confidential until then.

The Investiture will be held at Government House, Wellington, in May 1994 and my Official Secretary will advise you of the exact date as soon as this is confirmed.

Please accept my warmest congratulations.

Yours sincerely

Catherine Tizard

CATHERINE A TIZARD
Governor General

Mr Barry John Crump
c/- Wanaka Post Office
Wanaka
OTAGO

INVESTITURE
by
Her Excellency The Governor-General
Dame Catherine Tizard
at
Government House, Wellington
10.30 a.m. on Friday, 20th May, 1994

Recipient: *Barry Crump Esqre, M.B.E. (Civil)*

Recipients are requested to arrive by 10.00 am.

Dress: Ladies – Day Dress.
Gentlemen – Morning Dress,
Lounge Suit, or Uniform

PLEASE PRESENT THIS CARD ON ARRIVAL AT GOVERNMENT HOUSE

PRIME MINISTER

23 December 1993

Mr B J Crump
C/- Wanaka Post Office
Wanaka
OTAGO

Dear Mr Crump

Joan joins me in extending our congratulations on your recognition by Her Majesty The Queen in her 1994 New Year Honours.

Yours is a particularly fitting honour, recognising as it does, the valuable service you have given to your country. It is a tribute that I know will be welcomed by family and friends alike, as well as the wider community.

Yours sincerely

Rt Hon J B Bolger
Prime Minister

The Treasurer to
Their Royal Highnesses
The Prince and Princess of Wales
is commanded to invite
Mr. B. Crump
and Mrs. Crump
to a Garden Party to be given by
Their Royal Highnesses
at Government House, Auckland
on Monday, 25 April 1983, at 3.00 p.m.

Dress: Lounge Suit
Uniform
Day Dress

A reply is requested to:
The Director of Royal Visit,
P.O. Box 12-244,
Wellington North.

THIS IS NOT AN ADMISSION CARD

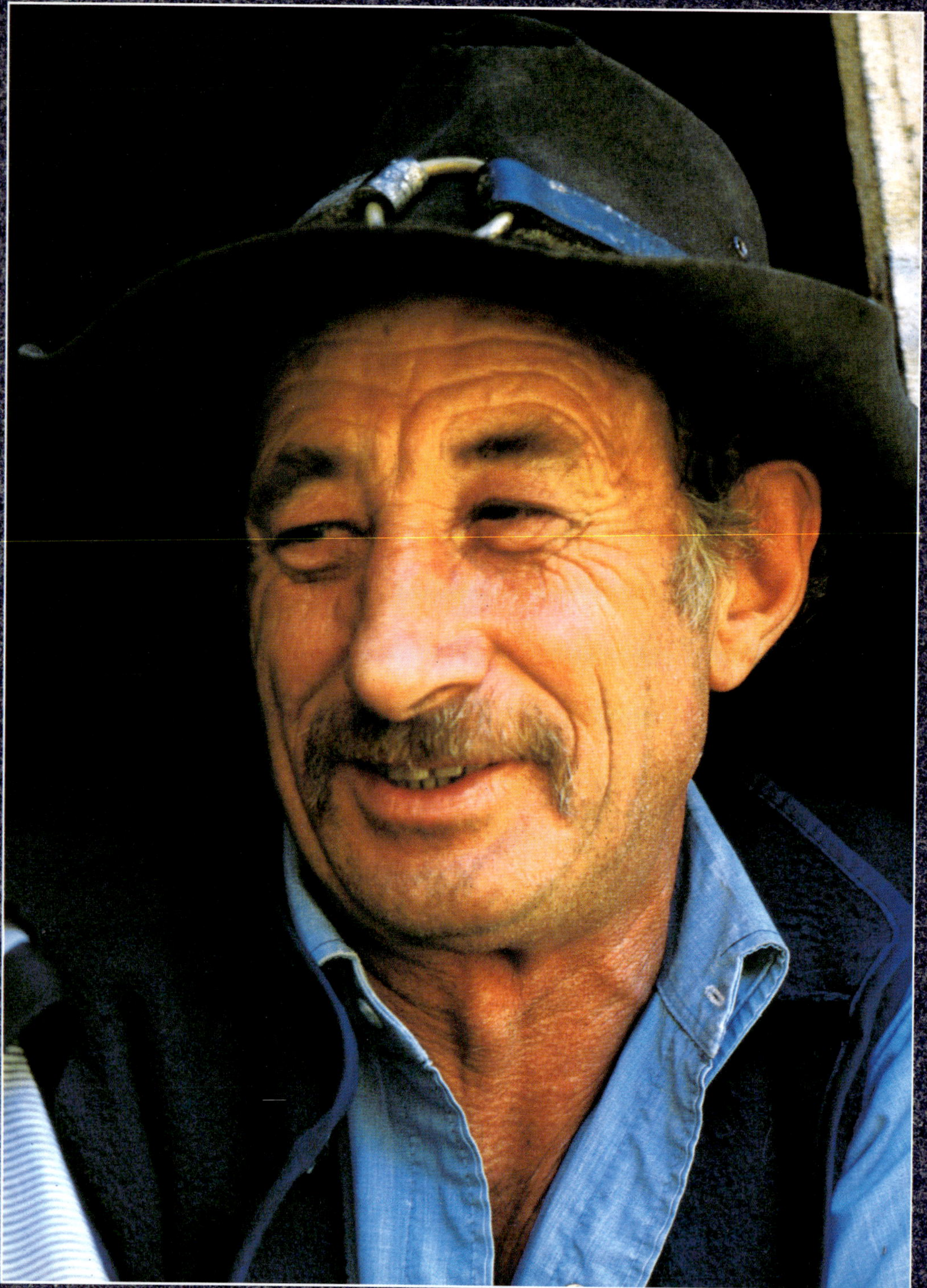

CHAPTER 7
WRITINGS

IN 1959 I STARTED WRITING MY FIRST BOOK, A GOOD KEEN MAN. MY GIRLFRIEND, JEAN, AND I WERE LIVING IN A POKY LITTLE BEDSITTER IN A BACK STREET AT THE TIME. JEAN WAS WORKING IN A PRINTERY AND I'D THROWN IN MY DRIVING JOB AND WORKED ON WHAT I JOKINGLY REFERRED TO AS "THE GREAT NEW ZEALAND NOVEL". I WROTE IT IN LONGHAND IN EXERCISE BOOKS AND THEN SPENT A MONTH PICKING IT OUT WITH TWO FOREFINGERS ON AN ANCIENT BORROWED IMPERIAL TYPEWRITER, ALTERING IT AS I WENT. I STILL WRITE THAT WAY, EXCEPT THE TYPEWRITER IS MORE UP-TO-DATE THESE DAYS.

– Forty Yarns and a Song

The poems included in this section are from Crumpy's notebooks. Some have been published previously. *Opportunity* is the first chapter in the book that Barry was working on when he died, titled *The Return of Sam Cash*. He was extremely excited about the novel, and said it would be his best ever.

Chapter 1
Opportunity

Sam Cash looked at the nearly bald bloke behind the desk without seeing him, and heard what he was saying without listening. Beyond the bloke, whose name Sam could never remember, he could see through the window the neat row of pensioner units. Maisy Burke was cutting some dahlias with a pair of scissors outside her unit, and old Pete Prendergast was sitting hunched on a kitchen chair in his doorway, both hands and his chin resting on his walking stick. Nick went past on the mower.

"This simply isn't good enough, Mr Cash," said the nearly bald bloke. "This business of the piano, now. You had no authority to move the piano in the first place, and Mrs Harcourt tells me that some of the songs you encouraged them to sing were – rather bawdy, to say the least. It simply isn't good enough, you were employed at Rest Hours as a gardener, not an entertainment officer – are you listening to me, Mr Cash?"

"Eh?" Sam ran his hands through his greying hair and tried to pay attention.

"I say this business of the piano. It isn't good enough."

"It was Rosy Dewar's birthday," said Sam.

"Well it's just not good enough," repeated the bloke. "You can't go shifting pianos around without authority. I'm afraid you've been something of a disruptive influence ever since you've been here Mr Cash."

"What do you keep the bloody piano for?" said Sam, bringing his attention back from wherever it had wandered. He found it hard to concentrate in these situations.

"The piano is provided for the use of our tenants on social occasions and such," said the bloke primly. "You can't just go shifting it around willy-nilly like that. It's just not . . ."

"Hang on a minute, mate," said Sam. "What the hell do you reckon someone's birthday is if it's not a social occasion? The trouble with you is that you don't like the idea of anyone enjoying themselves."

The bloke had both hands on his desk and a vein was throbbing in his neck.

"Excuse me," he said tightly. "You can't come in here talking to me like that. I'll have to remind you who you're talking . . ."

"Ar shut up, you miserable old bastard," said Sam calmly. "You're pretty good at telling people what they can't do, aren't you, mate. Well I'll tell you something you can do . . ."

And Sam told him, with the result that within an hour he was walking down the street with all he owned in a sports bag and a hundred and ten dollars in his pocket. He was glad to get out of that place. What he needed now was an opportunity.

"Got the price of a beer on you mate?" Wheezed the old bloke at Sam's elbow.

Sam looked at him. He knew that opportunity comes in all shapes and sizes but this one stretched even his imagination. The old bloke was scruffy and unkempt. He wore a suit that had once been expensive, now it was expiring. The shoulder pads of his coat were lumpy, the top pocket was torn down one side and there was a tear in one knee of his baggy pants. His shoes were so out of date that they were due to come back into fashion. A frayed brown shirt and a tie that had once been gaudy completed the ensemble, which had all the earmarks of having been purchased from the Salvation Army shop. On top of that he appeared to have a bruised cheekbone, a split lip and no top teeth. There was a smear of blood on the front of his shirt and he seemed to be wet all down one side. In short he was not an inspiring sight.

"What happened to you?" said Sam pushing money across the bar and motioning to the barman along the bar. "A truck run over you?"

"Nar," said the old bloke. "I got rolled by a couple of Maoris in the toilet of the other pub. They beat me up and took me pension money."

"I'm sorry chaps," said the barman, eyeing up the old bloke. "We've got a dress code in this bar. I'm afraid I can't serve you looking like that."

"Hang on a minute, mate," said Sam indignantly. "This bloke's just been beaten up and robbed. He needs a drink to settle his nerves before we take him up to the hospital. Give him a beer, and you'd better give him a whiskey as well, a double. In fact we'll both have one."

"Well just one then," said the barman reluctantly, reaching for glasses.

"Make mine a rum please," said the old bloke.

They took their drinks across to one of the tables.

"Now what's the story cobber?" said Sam.

The old bloke shakily drank from each of his drinks before replying.

"These two blokes followed me into the toilet and punched me up and then kicked me around," he said. "They broke me false teeth. I pretended to be out to it and they went through me pockets and took all me money. I think they've broken some of me ribs as well," he winced.

"Why didn't you go to the cops?" said Sam.

"Ah, it wouldn't be any use," said the old bloke. "I couldn't even recognise them. They had them black balaclavas pulled down over their faces. They were Maoris though, I could tell by the way they talked." He sculled his rum and drank again from his glass of beer.

"No clue who they might be?" asked Sam.

"Nar – except that one of them said no more drinking because they had to go out to Coopers to get his farm bike tonight, whoever Cooper is."

"That a fact?" said Sam thoughtfully.

Sam walked the old bloke along to a boarding house kind of place where he lived and gave him fifty of the ninety dollars he had left and told the woman there to get him cleaned up and put him into bed. Then Sam went back to the pub and asked the barman for a beer and the telephone book.

A car and trailer drove slowly along the road and as it came to the farm gateway its headlights went off. It rattled slowly across the cattle-stop and idled up the driveway, turned and backed the trailer up to the door of the implement shed. Two dark figures got out of the car and went to the shed. One of them inserted a pinch-bar in the lock and broke it off the door with a crack. They opened the door enough to let themselves in and then closed it again. A torch came on and shone around the shed on the bales of hay stacked at one end and then came to rest on the four-wheeled farm bike parked there.

"Here it is," whispered one of them. "She's a beauty, eh!"

"Let's wheel it out and get it on the trailer," said the other.

That was when their operation came to an abrupt halt. The shed lights came on and lit up the two young Maori blokes.

"Just stay right where you are, lads, and you won't get hurt," said Sam Cash informatively.

They spun round and saw Sam sitting on a bale of hay in the corner of the shed, one ankle across the other knee. He had a metal box in his lap with half a dozen wires leading away from it.

"Let's get out of here," said the shorter of the two, turning towards the door.

"Touch that door and I'll blow your sticky little fingers off for you," said Sam calmly.

The bloke reached out to open the door and there was a loud bang as Sam touched off one of the electric detonators he'd rigged up on the door. The two thieves stopped in their tracks, looking at the hole blown in the galvanised steel of the door.

"Let's get the old bastard," snarled the bigger one waving his pinch-bar menacingly towards Sam.

"Good idea," agreed Sam. "I'd like you to try that."

"You don't scare us," blustered the small one.

"I will in a moment," said Sam cheerfully.

"Come on," said the big one. "We'll get him."

The two thieves made for Sam and as they passed one each side of a bale of lucerne hay that was sitting in the middle of the floor it suddenly exploded in an ear-ringing blast that shook the whole building. The big bloke was flung against the wall, his pinch-bar clattering across the concrete floor, and the other one was sent sprawling into the farm bike they'd come to steal. The air inside the shed was thick with dust and particles of hay from the demolished bale.

The big bloke crawled a few feet on his hands and knees and then staggered to his feet, leaning on the wall. He was obviously concussed and completely disoriented. The other one sat on the floor whimpering, clutching at what looked to Sam like a broken arm. Sam took the plugs of cotton wool out of his ears and gave the two thieves enough time to gather what little wits they had left before he spoke.

"Now listen to me, lads. That was a quarter of a plug of molanite. That bike's got a whole plug of it under the seat, there's two more planted just outside the door and you car's parked right on top of four of them. One move out of either of you and I'll blow you to bloody bits."

"What are you going to do?" croaked the big bloke.

"We're going to stay right where we are like good little boys until the police get here," said Sam as though he was talking to backward children. "And we're going to think twice before we go kicking the snot out of an old bloke in a pub toilet, aren't we, you gutless pair of bastards."

The two thugs had nothing to say.

They waited in silence for another few minutes until the rake of headlights and the crunching of tyres on the gravel outside announced the arrival of a police car. Three policemen came cautiously into the shed.

"What's been going on here?" said the sergeant.

"I caught these two trying to swipe this farm bike." said Sam.

"We know them," said the sergeant. "Take them in, Harris."

The two other cops took the two very subdued thieves out to the police car and the sergeant said to Sam, "We've had our eye on those two and their mates for quite a while. How did you get on to them?"

"They beat up and robbed an old bloke called Herby Hocking in the pub this morning," said Sam. "He heard them talking about swiping someone's farm bike, so I rang around and found the place and jacked it up with the owner to head them off."

"Well good on you," said the sergeant, "but you should have come to us with it."

"Nar," grinned Sam. "You blokes would have taken all the fun out of it."

Fire

O Fire, what message
Have you imparted
To my vacant mind
As I stared those thousand hours
Into your gesticulating flames?

What wisdom have you whispered
To my unguarded ear
In your snapple and crack
And your muttering blaze?

Is the talk of Tawa wiser
Than the Rata or the Gum?
Is the sparkle of the Totara
More profound than either one?

Or are you just returning
Your substance to the sun,
And I just use its burning
On your smoking journey home?

O my servant, my companion,
Cook my food and warm my bed.
Dry my clothes and keep me cosy,
Keep me safe and keep me fed.

And yet I have heard fierce wars being fought
In the hunger of your conflagration
And seen Tyrannosaurus Rex wink at me
From the embers of your glowing grave.

Time of Day

At that time of day
when the world turns away from the sun
and the last traces of sunlight
are gone from the ridgetops,
I lead my old horse down a wild river valley
with two trout in the split sack
behind the saddle.

Around the bend I see great wires
strung swooping from pylon to pylon
across the sky.

And I wonder how come
it makes that moment of sadness
waft through my thoughts,
and puts that mournful note
in the cry of the putangitangi.

ODE TO A POLITICIAN

You claim to lead,
You're in the rear,
So where the hell
We go from here?

You take from us
As though you could
In this way do
Yourself some good.

This old folks' home
Please tell us why
Our aged are thrown
Out here to die.

That old man eating
Hand-out stew
Once saw his comrades
Die for you.

Ask that woman
What she did,
You'll find that she
Raised seven kids.

The mental patient
Sent away
Had with joy that very day
Her baby by the motorway.

My eyes can see
Your policy
Your words don't mean
A thing to me.

It's time, my friend,
For worthy deeds,
Homes and jobs
Are what we need.

Your record isn't good
My friend
And soon now
Your career will end.

And one day you'll be asked
To say
What you did when
You had your day.

If you would start
To earn my vote,
Give that old drunk
Your overcoat.

BAD BLUE

I got a dog off a bloke who was passing through
For a retread tyre and a beer or two,
It name and breeding no one knew
It was black and tan and I called him Blue, just Blue.

I took him home and, blast his hide,
He sank his teeth in my backside,
My trousers tore like a rotten sack,
I guess it doesn't pay to turn your back on Blue, not Blue.

I went out hunting and took this Blue
Just to see what he would do,
And he rounded an old boar pig,
Mean and lean and twice as big as Blue.

He ran that boar down a razor-back
And bailed him hard on a greasy track
They flattened fifty yards of scrub,
They wouldn't believe me in the pub about Blue.

Blue latched onto a nine-point stag
And it shook him out like a sleeping-bag,
That stag put on a mighty show
But he couldn't make that Blue let go, not Blue.

He shook the fleas off Blue's old hide
And dragged him down a shingle-slide.
He trampled Blue till his knees were weak
And tried to drown him in the creek, that Blue.

The stag gave up in sheer despair
And Blue hung on till I got there.
Killed that stag with my skinning-knife,
Best dog I had in all my life, that Blue.

Within a week I was in the gun
For all the damage he had done,
My wife she left me in despair
She wouldn't stay while Blue was there, not Blue.

He lost an ear and he lost an eye
I lost count of the scars on Blue's old hide.
He slipped his collar in my sleep
And killed eleven Romney sheep, Bad Blue.

Blue didn't die from poison-baits
Or rifle shots or bitten mates,
He didn't die from wounds or weather,
He ate my fowls and died of feathers, Poor Blue.

If there's a heaven where the good dogs go
I reckon Blue's been sent below,
And I'd like to see the sparks that flew
When the devil turned his back on Blue, Bad Blue.

Harry's Piece of Pain

Harry Roper found a bench and rested in the sun,
Studying his fellow man at shuffle, walk and run.
And as he watched with heavy-lidded gaze the bustle and the din,
All the voices died away but one that said, "Come in."

"Come in," it said. And then again, "Come in," he heard it say,
And though he waited patiently it wouldn't go away.
And then he saw the passing crowd move out across a plain,
Unable to resist the voice, "Come in," it said again.

He saw a shining mountain there, a door was open wide,
He saw the people shed their cares and start to move inside.
And very soon a multitude was flowing in and past
And Harry knew that humankind was coming home at last.

Everyone who ever lived, from everywhere on earth
Was heading for the mighty door, regardless of their worth.
From every long and latitude, from every tribe they came,
And everyone who entered there was greeted by their name.

And as they passed within the door, the lame were made to walk,
The blind were made to see again, the dumb were made to talk.
The guilty left their fear outside like rows of muddy boots,
And very soon the plain was strewn with faulty attributes.

The rich were made to shed the load they'd carried all their lives,
The parted were united with their husbands and their wives.
The poor were lifted from the road they'd trodden all their days,
The heedless lifted up their eyes in gratitude and praise.

Humble, worn and sick at heart, and weary of the fight,
They heard the voice that said, "Come in," and hurried to the light.
And when at last they'd all gone in and left him on the plain,
He gazed arund the empty world and hung his head in shame.

He saw across an oily sea great smears of greed and gain,
And over on the other side was loss and want and pain.
All the ignorance of man was there to see, and yet
The only thing that Harry felt was sadness and regret.

And now he hadn't any choice, no time to lose or win,
He had to turn and face the voice that said once more, "Come in."
And as he moved towards the door he wept because he'd seen
A better life he could have lived, the way it should have been.

They found old Harry sitting there, a dribble on his chin,
They put him in a wooden box and said a prayer for him.
They lowered him into the ground, the place from whence he'd come,
They stood and thought, the score of life? When added up, what sum?

CUP OF TEA

Sitting with my sister and a milky cup of tea,
Talking chat of this and that, a thought comes over me.
I suddenly remember some of how I've spent my time,
And I see a few occasions where I've wandered out of line.

Life at home among the family saw me oft across the knee,
And some of that, I reckon, could have been because of me.
And I must have been a nuisance to the teachers at the schools,
It might have turned out better if I'd understood the rules.

The lies I told the ladies, the ones I told in court
Were mainly only borrowed from the things that I'd been taught.
And other bits of mischief that crop up inside my head –
Perhaps the only reason is because I'm easy-led.

I could put it down to ignorance and maybe ease my mind,
But I could have given Peter more than twenty bucks that time.
I can't remember what I've lost, or had ripped off from me,
But I can't forget those boots I stole when I was twenty-three.

Though it's not the indicretions of the past that bug me now,
It's the ones I keep repeating that still bother me somehow.
I know, as years go tumbling by, we'll all come right at last,
But have I got sufficient years to tidy up my past?

I see the things I need to change, how simple it all seems,
Such little things have kept me from fulfilling all my dreams,
But then this though is very shy, a timid reverie –
I blink away the whole display, my sister says, "More tea?"

JOURNEY

The hand that felled and split the tree
And sank the posts in sand and scree
And strung the wire and battened-up,
Now raps the saucer with the cup.

The arm that slung the hauler-spragg
And sprung the breech and strung the stag
And swung the jangling ploughing team,
Now reaches out to play the queen.

The ear that heard the south wind roar
And smash the vessel on the shore
And heard the names of shipmates read,
Now hardly hears what's being said.

The foot that trod the frozen clay
And kicked the winning goal that day;
The foot that once wore hide and steel,
Now puts its slippers on by feel.

The soul that since before its birth,
Now weary of its term on earth
And quickened by a glimpse of light,
Rejoices, and prepares for flight.

PHOTOGRAPH CREDITS

Andrew Campbell
Pages 93, 94

Barry Crump Collection
Pages: 9, 10, 17, 18, 19, 22, 23, 24, 25, 28, 29, 30, 32, 33, 35, 36, 37, 39, 40, 41, 42, 46, 47, 48, 52, 53, 54, 57, 60, 73, 75, 80, 82, 90, 100, 103, 104, 105, 108, 109, 110, 111, 113, 114, 115, 120, 128, 132, 136, 137, 148, 149, 151, 152, 153, 158, 160, 172, 173, 174, 176, 177, 178, 179, 187, 195, 196, 197, 198

Alex King
Pages: 141, 143, 196

New Zealand Herald
Pages: 44, 56, 62, 65, 71, 78, 81, 95, 97, 99, 118, 123, 131, 134, 163

New Zealand Listener
Page 77

News Media
Pages: 83, 159

Simone Rainger
Page 102

Andrew Scott
Pages: 12, 38, 50, 66, 89, 162, 166, 171

Sally Tagg
Pages: 15, 16, 20, 21, 106, 107, 116, 117, 146, 147

Toyota New Zealand
Pages: 11, 164, 165, 167, 168, 169

We have received photographs from many sources and have endeavoured wherever possible to acknowledge the copyright holder. We apologise for any omissions and would like to thank all contributors for making their photographs available to us.